GREAT OR PC

GREAT OR POOR

'Satisfied' customers are not enough

Guy Arnold

2000

First published in 2011 by Management Books 2000 Ltd
Forge House, Limes Road
Kemble, Cirencester
Gloucestershire, GL7 6AD, UK
Tel: 0044 (0) 1285 771441
Fax: 0044 (0) 1285 771055
Email: info@mb2000.com
Web: www.mb2000.com

British Library Cataloguing in Publication Data is available

ISBN 9781852526931

CONTENTS

WARNING

The principles and tools in this piece of work are very powerful and effective. If they are not used with integrity, they can be very manipulative.

This will ruin these ideas for others: please only use this material with Integrity!

PREFACE

Thanks for buying this book.

This work has come about by mistake and trial and error, but it's been through the mill and the ideas within it tested in many different organisations and situations.

I love the Chinese proverb:

> *'Give a man a fish and you feed him for a day;*
> *teach him how to fish and you feed him for a lifetime.'*

This is a book to teach people 'how to fish' – how to put simple principles to work, at any level in any organisation, to deliver consistently excellent customer experiences, and, by doing this, make those organisations more productive, better places to work, more innovative and, of course, much more profitable.

If you're a leader or manager, there'll be some great ideas that you can take away and put into place in your organisation instantly. If you're not a leader or manager, there are great ideas here that you can start to apply in your role, and thereby grow your effectiveness and influence for your own present success and career growth.

The world is changing very fast: those that delight the customer best are the winners, and those that consistently evolve around and grow the customers' real and future needs will continue to be winners. Standing still in any role or organisation is not an option.

The Internet is empowering customers of both private and public organisations like never before: the 21st Century is truly a new age of empowered customers and transparent business.

And please be aware: there's a HUGE gap between 'customer service' and 'customer experience'; they are 2 different sides of the same coin. The customer isn't interested in your 'service', they're interested in their 'experience'. This 'experience' will then be spread by them to the world and becomes 'the word on the street'.

The word on the street will determine your future success or failure; it's as simple as that. Your 'service' may deliver great experiences, or may not; you won't know unless you find out!

All this is, of course, blindingly obvious common sense, and it's fair to say that everyone (well, almost everyone) wants to both receive and give great experiences; that's what life is all about, and that's what makes people and organisations successful.

So the real issue is: **why doesn't it happen each and every time?**

This is the question I couldn't find an answer to, and which led me to researching this issue and, by mistake, writing this book. This book seeks to answer that question, and give you the answers and tools, based on simple principles of common sense, to empower you to address it start being more successful.

Some cultures around the world have a reputation of being better at 'customer service' than others, but even those countries where great customer experiences are common have many opportunities to improve — and, of course, there are other countries where the customer experience is perhaps still a secondary or tertiary consideration for many organisations.

Whatever your position and wherever you're starting, remember that success is a journey; **if you can be a little bit better tomorrow than you were today, then that's a success**. This book is based on simple principles of common sense that I hope will make it easy to understand. But, as is often the case with common sense, it can be easier to understand than do, because we live in a somewhat dysfunctional world ... and life can get in the way!

But remember, knowledge without action is pointless. The key point I make in the 3rd principle is *'Go the Extra Inch'*; any action and progress is better than none. Don't worry about taking small steps ... small consistent steps multiplied by time can equal great success over time!

Go for it and very good luck!

....

A piece of advice: 'customer experience' is NOT all about 'being nice'; it's about the whole customer journey from marketing, to contact, to sale, to continuing relationship and after sale. These principles apply to all these areas. So please don't think, 'I'm in IT, or Administration, or Finance, or Marketing (or whatever), so this isn't a book for me.' This is a book based on life principles (that are all, of course, common sense), to empower you to be successful with both internal and external customers, whatever your role.

So it applies to everyone ... doing everything!

....

Lastly, a word of thanks: this has been quite a tough journey to get off the ground, mainly for those around me. Thank you to my family, customers and friends who have believed in me and helped me complete this project – in particular my wife Alison and my father Simon who have always been a particular source of strength and support.

And, very importantly, I feel obliged to point out that this is NOT all my thinking ... I have drawn inspiration from many great teachers: through their work and lives. Everything here is 'blindingly obvious common sense' ... All I have tried to do is pull this common sense together into an organised system, so everyone can read and learn, and, through this work, aim to start applying and using these proven principles for their own personal success in their role.

INTRODUCTION

Great or poor is an idea born out of frustration:

- frustration of business owners: who are struggling to build their business, know they ought to get help from outside advisers, but don't want to be charged a fortune for complicated advice or pricey systems, that will often make their lives harder
- frustration of managing directors: who need to deliver the numbers to their stakeholders, but can't seem to get the buy in and commitment from their people
- frustration of managers: who traditionally feel they ought to find answers to all the business conundrums that come their way, but are often out of their depth, and, while trying to appear strong, they struggle below the surface
- frustration of workers: who want to do a good job, but often feel disempowered, disenfranchised, and frustrated in their roles
- frustration of stakeholders: who can't understand why things don't happen as they planned
- frustration of customers: who often get a poor deal at inflated prices, and so feel frustrated and 'untrusting' of companies they deal with
- my personal experience of frustration as a business owner and business adviser: when I see that 'blindingly obvious common sense' is so often not common practice

This work helps resolve all these conundrums, and helps people at all levels to deliver consistently excellent customer experiences ... day in, day out ... no matter what.

Because this is what your customer is actually paying for!

Your product or service is basically irrelevant. Your customer is not buying your product or service. **Your customer is buying the experience or feeling that your product or service gives to them.**

And in today's truly global market, where supply outstrips demand, innovation and competition arise in an instant, and your customers are truly empowered via the Internet to make or break you, *you now have no choice:*

- You have to be consistent in your quality, value and service (for this is the make-up of the customer 'experience')
- And you have to keep continually and obsessively looking for and implementing ways to improve and grow.

Because, if you don't, you'll be dead in the water sooner or later.

So, the overriding aim to deliver consistently excellent customer experiences must be the number one goal of every organisation in the 21st Century that wants to thrive or even survive.

Remember Darwin's law:

> *'It is not the strongest of the species that survives, but those most adaptable to change.'*

And the world of business is littered with the corpses of once great organisations to prove the point ...

So, you'd think that all organisations would have a powerful, simple and foolproof system to ensure this always happened, and their customers would either receive a consistently excellent experience, or at least be able to converse with the organisation to sort it out when it goes wrong, wouldn't you?

The incredible thing is that the vast majority of organisations do not have an effective SYSTEM in place. Yes, lots of people ask for 'customer feedback' or run periodic 'satisfaction surveys', but we all know as customers that this isn't enough.

(In fact, these are often even worse than the initial problem!)

What is needed is a SYSTEMATIC approach to this whole issue to ensure that the *whole organisation or team is effectively aligned around the overriding goal of delivering consistently great customer experiences as the single biggest organisational goal* … no matter what – and the only way to do this is to 'begin with the end in mind' of achieving this goal, and then work back to align all strategy, systems, processes, and measures (and, by default therefore, behaviour) around this overriding 'mission'.

But, don't worry, Rome wasn't built in a day. I know that most people reading this cannot reorganise everything overnight. The key is to remember that this is the 'mission' and then to START changing around this 'mission'. This book will show you how to do this.

You cannot change your situation today, but you can change your destination …

So, back to systems:

Business effectiveness is a product of behaviour within systems.

So what systems do you have to effectively manage, improve and measure your customer's experience of your goods and services?

My guess is … not enough – and this is why all the above issues arise. Organisations can only thrive and grow in the long term if they deliver excellent customer experiences consistently and systematically.

If you don't have systems to measure and manage this, how can you possibly thrive and grow? At best it will be luck or perhaps the actions of a few outstanding individuals carrying the rest along.

You need a system!

Great or Poor is a simple and effective system to help you consistently deliver excellent customer experiences, throughout your organisation each day, every day no matter what your position.

I wrote this book because, in a former role as a Director of a FTSE 100 Company, tasked with putting together a policy and process to improve the customer experience, despite attending non stop seminars and reading a mountain of 'customer service' books, all I got was a huge list of 'top tips' and things to do ... most of which I already knew because they were blindingly obvious common sense. So I decided to research this properly, and by mistake, it turned into the book you're reading now!

My research started by asking just one question:

'If customer service is common sense, why is it so often not common practice?'

And progressed, when I found some answers, to:

'And what can an organisation do to TRULY address this in a systematic way?'

This book is not a list of top tips and ideas.

We have all read books and come away from training courses with great lists of ideas of behaviours and things to do ... and how many have we actually put into practice?

Not very many?

So why is this? We'll answer that question in full later on, but, in general I think it boils down to two overriding issues:

- Because it's 'common sense' most people assume (often mistakenly) that it'll automatically be 'common practice'... And we all know as customers how mistaken this assumption can be!
- You can take a horse to water, but you cannot make it drink. Most customer service work focuses on instructing people to do things that are 'blindingly obvious common sense', which so often has the opposite effect of putting them off doing these things!

This 'common sense' actually needs to be managed effectively through a system (of course)!

In writing *Great or Poor*, I have looked for 'the simplicity on the far side of complexity'. What I mean by this is that, if you study any subject long enough, consider every issue through the focus of one question, 'what is common sense?', then link everything via this question (and discard anything that doesn't comply with it), eventually you should come up with material that is common sense, simple, and powerful.

We have managed to distil, through thirty years of experience, and four years of research, study and testing, some key ideas and habits, that will produce outstanding customer experiences (no matter what your role, and no matter who your customer, or customers, are) into **4 simple principles**.

We believe that *the only way that a business can consistently deliver excellence is to do a few simple things very, very well.*

Simple things done well is far better than complicated things done averagely.

People cannot remember complicated lists, or detailed strategies (that often change regularly), but they can remember and consistently apply **four simple, clear, empowering, basic principles of common sense**.

If any business, organisation, team, or individual takes and applies these four principles to their situation, we guarantee you will see significant improvements in results over time.

If you do not, please send this book back to us, with a short covering note, and we will refund your money.

Thank you for taking the time to read this and if you enjoy it and find value in it please pass the details on, and ask others to buy it and share it.

(P.S. If you also want to put a customer review on Amazon or share a link to www.greatorpoor.com via your website or social media, that'd be fantastic as well!)

1

BASIC PRINCIPLES

'The opposite of love is not hate, it is indifference'
George Bernard Shaw

I will start by telling you the meaning of a couple of words. The two words I'd like to tell you about, that I've used already, are 'simple' and 'effective'.

Simple – 'simple' is so important because most customer service material isn't 'simple', it's complicated and people are surprised when they go away and go back to their jobs and things don't happen.

So this is a simple system that anyone can remember and anyone can apply.

The second word is **'effective'** – now 'effective' means two things:

1. doing the right things, and
2. doing them in the right way.

This system enables you to do both of those things.

So rather than telling you a load of old stuff you already know (which people find annoying at best ... and insulting at worst), we are telling you how to make the common sense of what you already know **actually happen** all day, everyday.

What's the REAL issue with 'customer service'? Well, I think it can be summed up as follows:

1. Every organisation wants it's customers to recommend them to their friends, and return for future and additional purchases
2. Every member of staff gets out of bed in the morning wanting to make a success of the day

3. Every (well almost every) customer wants to have a good experience

So, logically, great service should happen as a matter of routine. Yet, somehow, things just don't seem to happen this way!

This is called 'The Execution Gap', and everyone wants to bridge it. Yet every business is different, and every customer (both internal and external) has different needs.

Now, through the power of the Internet, an upset customer can severely damage your business overnight.

On top of this, because supply outstrips demand, innovation and technology have combined to give customers amazing experiences as standard, and competition springs up overnight, often from a part of the world with much lower fixed costs, 'customer satisfaction' is now close to worthless ... it's 'customer loyalty' that is the key business advantage for the 21st century. In a nutshell, our view is that

'satisfied' customers are not good enough; in their opinion you are either 'great' or 'poor'

...and there's not much in between.

Not only this, but when you're 'OK' then customers will be 'indifferent' to you. They won't ruin you, but they won't promote you ... and over time they'll drift away, leaving you with no option but to spend large sums on marketing to fill their place.

A few decades ago, in general, demand outstripped supply (as it had done since the start of the Industrial Revolution). This has now changed ...

... the world is a VERY different place!

To be successful, you have two choices:

1. Reduce your prices so you're the cheapest (which works well as long as you can deliver HUGE volume ... and until someone cheaper comes along)

2. Improve your customer experience, so you are delivering more 'value' ... thus growing your business through increased order sizes, repeat business, cross sales and referrals.

The Internet has now empowered your customers like never before – customers are more and more demanding ... everyone wants more for less! Most people would never book a hotel today without checking on a hotel feedback website first. Ebay could not function without customer feedback. This same thinking will, very shortly, apply to all business and personal transactions.

The Customer really is king in the 21st Century

This is really good news.

If your customers think you are 'great', your business will grow through repeat sales, cross sales, referrals, increased order sizes, and your costs will fall as you have less problems to sort out, more innovation and less need for large sales and marketing budgets.

There is of course a downside.

If your customers think you are 'poor', then your business will shrink and die as your competition continues to improve, as the only way to drive sales will be through expensive sales and marketing campaigns, combined with high costs of doing business.

When you've lost a customer it's very, very, hard to get them back, and, as previously mentioned, all of this has now become CRITICALLY important to business survival, as the power of social media grows and grows.

The only way to long term success is to delight your customers by delivering consistently excellent (or, at the very least, 'consistent') customer experiences each time, every time, at all levels, and no matter who is in charge.

This is of course easier to understand than do!

Our research indicates that in many cases this isn't happening and you as a customer know that is true. This results in reduced sales, reduced margins, increased costs, high levels of frustration and disengagement in people and lack of business growth and profit in the long term.

Sometimes, businesses can grow through

- innovation,
- exploiting a gap or opportunity in the market,
- high energy management,
- outstanding personality and leadership,
- cost reduction cutting things 'close to the bone'
- great marketing, brand building and sales efforts
- and, sometimes, even by treating people badly and misleading customers

but, always, this is short-term, and without excellent customer experiences consistently delivered, the long-term will be bleak.

Systems make things happen consistently.

So, every business needs a system to ensure that the customer experience is delivered consistently and excellently, no matter who's in charge, no matter what the budget is, no matter what the external financial situation is, no matter what the weather's like, and no matter what mood the boss is in!

This book will deliver you a simple and effective system to achieve this and the advice around it will help you to deliver excellence as standard and give you and your people:

- the **knowledge** to know what excellent customer service looks like,
- the **skills** to enable them to do it and
- the **attitude** to want to deliver it

because you have to have all three to make this a habit that is consistently applied throughout your organisation.

If it isn't a habit, constantly reinforced by your systems, *it won't happen.*

Customer service is not an event, or a behaviour, it's a series of habits, reinforced by systems, practised by everyone, every day at every level in an organisation. We have all heard the phrase 'a chain is only as good as it's weakest link', and this is of course true with customer service – every link must be strong and aligned.

This system also will tell you how good your service has to be, especially in tough times, what actually stops it from happening and what to do about it, and really importantly, how you measure it effectively.

Incredibly this doesn't cost much to do, but it costs a fortune not to do. It does however take belief, perseverance, passion and integrity.

Some good news:

It's easy to understand!

Some bad news:

It's not a quick fix ... it will take persistence & integrity!

This book will give you an overview of the main points, some examples that fit in with those points and enable you to take action.

One thing I must say is that please read this again and again. Do not just read this once and say, 'I've done that, lets move on'. It's like listening to a song and saying, 'I really liked that song but I'm never going to listen to it again.' You'd want to listen to it again and again and again. Repetition will make this system happen automatically.

When you've done this:

TAKE SOME ACTION

Start with little steps – change one thing this week, and then one the next, and on and on! It will work! *Any positive change and action is better than doing nothing.* Then keep reviewing and rereading this material, and keep on making small and systematic changes. If you then review this after a month, 6 months and a year, you'll be amazed at the progress you've made!

I cannot reinforce this strongly enough – this is NOT a quick fix! There is no such thing (don't believe what those adverts for face cream say on the TV!), this is a systematic approach to the main issue and opportunity for business in the 21st Century ... and it's long overdue!

> *'Madness is doing the same things and expecting different results.'*
> Albert Einstein

We can offer you further information, weekly top tips, new articles and free resources on our websites, *www.greatorpoor.com* and *www. gotheextrainch.org*.

And of course we'd like to work with you if you want to improve you customer experience so if you like this and other material that we publish please do contact us, for a no obligation chat to see what we can do to help you become more successful.

Background

So first of all we'll start of with an introduction, and I'd like to tell you a small amount about myself without boring you to tears.

My background is as a business trouble-shooter. I used to go into businesses that were bankrupt, closed or struggling, and I'd rearrange them, turn them around and sell them on. Most of my experience has been in the licensed and leisure industry and for a long time I did this for other people.

Then one day, when my wife and I were newly married, I said to her, 'Why on earth are we doing this for other people, lets do it for ourselves!' So we moved to Devon and bought a bankrupt pub and small hotel on the edge of Dartmoor, a beautiful place, and we did exactly the same thing.

But I had a vision there, an inspiration I should say, and it was all due to my wife Alison.

I was working behind the bar one day, doing all the things I had told people to do, I had rearranged the way the place worked, all the systems, the purchasing, the marketing, I'd made it attractive to people, but I was so obsessed with making all this stuff happen that I'd forgotten to be nice to the customers – I wasn't smiling when someone walked through the door.

My wife pulled me aside, and said, 'Guy, you are forgetting the single most important thing. People can put up with the menus not being perfect, the blackboards not being written, they can put up with things not being quite just so. *What people cannot put up with is not feeling welcome.*'

To me that was a complete revelation.

From that moment I became obsessed with asking myself, 'Why is it that this obvious thing gets missed by so many people? Even me, as a business trouble shooter, running my own business had missed it!'

So, many years later, after extensive thought, research and testing, here is my simple and effective answer to that simple and frustrating question ... combined with what you need to do in order to make it happen for you.

Health warning

I would like give you a warning here. Please if you are not prepared to take action then stop reading now because **knowledge without action equals frustration** ... for everyone you interact with. You need to be prepared to take one or two key steps from this material and actually do them.

You have to ask yourself:

'How am I going to push myself out of my comfort zone and change?'

Because what I'm going to tell you here is like explaining to you the location of a gold mine. If I came to you one day and said,

'Hey, I've got this gold mine, it's fantastic, I've got so much gold up there I can't keep digging it. Anyone who comes up with a shovel and a wheelbarrow can dig it, they can just have it because there's too much for me. I'll tell you where it is and I'll tell you how to get it and I'll even tell you how to dig it but you've got to come, you've got make the journey and you've got to buy your own equipment.'

Many people will say, 'I'd love to but I just haven't got the time', or 'Have you seen how much shovels cost?' or 'I don't know, it's a bit far out of my way to get to that goldmine.'

So just ask yourself, are you prepared to see this as a goldmine?

Because if you do it will be. But if you see it as a 'bit of a chore' that gets in the way of 'real business', then it will be that as well. **Whatever you believe will be true!**

Systems

Systems are very important, *systems make things work.*

If you go into McDonalds in New York it will be the same as McDonalds in Delhi and the same as McDonalds in Moscow. The reason for this is: everything has a system.

I am not advocating complete uniformity and lack of individual creative input in customer service ... often quite the opposite. But, in order to produce a consistent customer experience, the business has to be driven at its core by systems. This will then empower your people to 'go the extra inch' to deliver a great customer experience and help your organisation improve and grow.

"SAUSAGE + CHIPS, THAT'S WHAT THE PLOUGHMAN HAS FOR LUNCH."

What I am presenting to you here is a simple system which, if you adopt it, will dramatically improve your customer service. Be that for yourself as an individual, for your team, for your department or for your whole organisation, depending on the level you are. It also works at home, it works for not-for-profit organisations, it works whether the organisation is large or small, it works in the public sector and it works in the private sector.

Common sense

The reason why it works is it's a system based on common sense and *common sense contains the key rules of life that happen whether we like it or not!*

For example, if an apple falls from a tree it will fall to the ground. It's common sense. Gravity works whether we like it or not. There is nothing we can do about it. We can accept that gravity is there and work our lives around it or we can choose to fight against it, which isn't a great recipe for success ...

Likewise there are key principles of human behaviour and interaction that apply in the world whether we like it or not – these are found in all the great religions, and everything you'll read here will be what I call: *Blindingly Obvious Common Sense!*

But, as we know, the REAL problem is that so often common sense is not common practice!

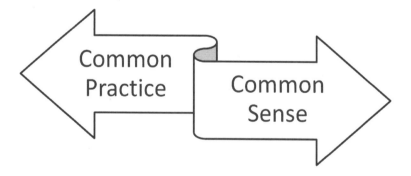

What we present here is a system that works with the common sense principles of life, that if you adopt it, you ally yourself to the great force of common sense, the force of life, to help you be great at whatever you do, and thus deliver outstanding customer experiences consistently and excellently.

Just before we get into the actual system I would like to tell you about an article I read recently called, 'The £15 billion annual cost of poor customer service'. It goes like this:

> Poor customer service costs UK businesses more than £15 billion a year. With telecommunications, utilities and financial service companies said to be the biggest losers. According to this survey the cost of poor customer service is now such a significant issue and most companies are losing significant business through customers defecting and abandoning their purchases as a direct result of unsatisfactory service experiences. These same businesses say it costs too much to train people so they put CRM (Customer Relationship Management) systems in place to try and do the job instead and spend billions trying to get new customers via huge sales and marketing budgets.

This is complete lunacy.

And here's a Quote from a National Consumer Council report called 'The Stupid Company':

> It can be easy for commentators and campaigners to conclude that businesses are on occasion simply malicious in their treatment of customers. But our work reveals that, all too often, companies harm themselves. By turning consumers against them, companies neglect their own self-interest, damaging their profits and in some cases leading to their demise. We call this remarkable phenomenon 'the stupid company.' There are many committed and well-intentioned people working in business, and lots of truly inspiring entrepreneurs, but all too often companies as institutions behave in a way that is completely counter-productive. This is not only bad for consumers and companies, but damaging for the competitiveness of our economy.

All of the above is, of course, a statement of the blindingly obvious, we all know as customers how often we feel undervalued and abused. But **the key to business success is to create a system of ongoing excellence for delivery and continual improvement that makes it easier to deliver great customer experiences than not deliver them.**

Principles of common sense

Before we get into the system I'd like to talk about the ideas and principles of customer service as background – I look at this as a bit like building the foundations.

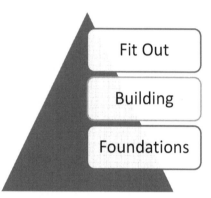

When you build a house you spend a long time on the foundations, and when people walk past the building site they often wonder, 'When are they ever going to build that house?' And when they start building ... whoosh, it goes up almost overnight. But the most important thing, the thing that takes the time and the thing that takes the effort, is the foundations. *Without good foundations the house will fall over!*

So we'll start by talking about the foundational ideas and principles and then we'll move onto the system.

The first thing I'd like to do is ask you to think about some questions. The first question is:

Do you think in your business 'good' is good enough?

I would like you to pause and consider that question for a while. Maybe write some thoughts below:

(Note: if you believe the answer is 'yes, 'good' is good enough', then just take a time to consider your business 1 to 5 years from now – where will your competition come from? What will your customers be demanding? What will 'good' look like then? Remember, 'pride comes before a fall'.)

Customers expect more than 'good'. Customers expect a 'great' experience – they are empowered by the Internet, and compare your experience to that delivered by **every other person or business** they interact with, whether they are your competitors or not. You have world class competition all over the place!

So, if you make a 'good' effort in your business, is it perhaps logical to presume that you'll only get an 'OK' reaction from a customer, because customers are demanding?

So being 'good' will only give you an OK result. This is getting more and more the case in the world today. The internet is empowering the customer like never before, the economy is becoming completely global, I can speak to someone in India just as easy as someone in London. The credit bubble we have been through shows how reckless spending has got people into trouble and for a long time people will remember that and be much more cautious about how they spend their money.

So you've got to keep improving, you've got to be 'great' rather than 'good'.

The second question I'd like you to think about for a few minutes is:

What do you think your customers actually crave from you?

Please take some time to consider this, and maybe write some thoughts in below:

Would it be fair to say that your **customers expect you to deliver what you say you're going to do as a very minimum?**

What they actually crave is to be 'treated valuably'. To be cared about, to be given valuable attention, to be treated as a human being. You've got to ask yourself, 'Are we focusing so much on delivering the basics that we are forgetting the absolutely crucial part of **treating people valuably**?'

Why bother? We're currently doing OK ...

So why bother? Surely if you're OK at the moment and not focusing on the customer experience isn't hurting your profits, (who are you trying to kid?) – why do you have to bother about this stuff?

It might be fair to say that you may be OK (or even 'great') at the moment, things may be going fine but, as mentioned above, consider what I've just said: the internet is empowering the customer, the economy is truly global. What you are 'great' at today could be just the thing that someone else, on the other side of the world, is working hard at trying to steal from you, or try a new innovative approach, without your knowledge, with much lower overheads, and no baggage, in order to take your market away from you.

Competition today arises overnight.

You have to keep moving forward, otherwise you are, by definition, moving backward.

The more profit you're making today, the more likely it is that competition will already be planning on ways to take it away from you.

The power of money

Money does not actually exist.

Money derives it's power from a universal 'buy-in' into it's effectiveness as a 'measure of barter or trade'. It is, of course, a fantastic measure – it powers the capitalist world. But it is a phenomenally short-sighted measure as well (and we have all seen the awful consequences of this short-sightedness in the recent global recession, and ongoing with the wanton destruction of our environment in the name of 'profit today' (and 'never mind tomorrow'!)).

Money is usually measured, in essence, by 'profit'.

Profit is a great measure of 'success today'.

But profit can often be achieved at the expense of 'success tomorrow'.

The 'customer experience' is the measure of 'success tomorrow'.

Because the 'customer experience' today will drive the customer buying habits tomorrow (BOCS again of course, but only while I was writing this did I overhear this snippet of conversation: 'This is business ... be ruthless' – and how often have we experienced this as customers?).

Money is just a measure of 'energy'. It's a very important measure, and it makes many things happen. But, as many found out in the recent global recession, it can disappear as fast as it arrives, and there are other sources of energy that should not be dismissed in the mad quest for money. Of course the most powerful of these, and getting more powerful every day, is the 'customer experience' ... which is manifested through what they say about you and your services behind your back.

The organisations that flourish in a recession are those that consistently deliver a great customer experience. This is because of 3 main reasons:

1. Existing customers stay with them through thick and thin
2. New customers come to them because economic necessity has made them more demanding
3. They can react to changing economic circumstances much more quickly because they're closer to their customers.

The 'customer experience' is sometimes called: 'the word on the street'.

Well managed, the word on the street can be harnessed to drive your business forward. Poorly managed (or, what is more commonplace, not managed at all and left to chance), it can severely harm you or destroy you overnight.

Unfortunately, *people are much keener to talk about 'poor' experiences than 'great' experiences* ... at least 10 times more.

(Incidentally, social media is beginning to redress this balance, as consumers are positively sharing great experiences to help others, so this reinforces the great opportunity of getting this right).

So you have to be 'great', or else your 'poor' experiences can ruin your organisation. (And remember, whether the customer's opinion is 'true' or not is irrelevant – if it's their 'experience' it'll be true for them. These are called 'moments of truth', of which more later).

Unfortunately, no matter how 'great' you are, 'poor' experiences will always happen, because nobody is perfect.

If you are generally just 'satisfactory', then there is not enough customer loyalty in your business or brand to get you through these problems. If you are 'great' you will have enough goodwill built up to rectify the issue (because they'll usually tell you, rather than telling all their friends) and retain the customer's loyalty.

If we accept that money is energy, then your 'customer experience' must deliver significantly more energy to your customer (from the customer's point of view) than the energy it cost your customer to acquire it.

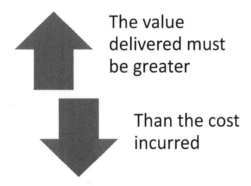

The value delivered must be greater

Than the cost incurred

Price competition
Sometimes I'm accused of talking soft and fluffy nonsense, and

1. 'it's tough out there'
2. 'in reality it's not like that'
3. 'price is more important than service'

To which I reply (in order):

1. 'Yes, that's why it's so important to get this right: – the worse you do this, the tougher it will be for you'
2. 'Reality is what you make it :
   a. If your attitude is 'I'll believe it when I see it' (the great 'glass half empty' view), then you'll be right:.
   b. If your attitude is 'I'll see it when I believe it (the great 'glass half full' view) then you'll be right.
   c. Give it a go – if it's so awful 'out there' then surely things can't get any worse!'
   d. I love the quote from Henry Ford, and have it stuck on my office wall: ***"if you think you can, or you think you can't, you're probably right".*** Great!
3. 'Yes, price is important, you always have to charge a fair price **for the long term**, but it's ONLY more important than service when there are no other discerning factors.'
   • If your customer trades with you purely because of your price, what they are really telling you is that your service could do with some improvement!
   • What will then happen when someone with lower overheads and better systems suddenly starts to undercut you?

Some more views on price, before we move on:

• If price is your 'unique selling proposition', then, in reality, you haven't got a unique selling proposition (unless you're a business like Poundland)
• People who trade on price rip you off, pay late, steal your ideas and mess you around ... don't go for them ... go for the sensible majority who want a 'great' experience at a 'fair' price!
• If you win business on price, then you'll lose it on price – the ONLY long term factor for success is great customer service, producing customer loyalty.
   – There was a fantastic example of this recently in the Uk, when a 'Poundland' shop was put out of business by a 99p shop next door!

- Be transparent on price. If you're more expensive, be open and tell your customers why – they'll often opt for the more expensive but more transparent option (because it engenders trust). Some examples of this:
  - Amazon.com: tell you all the different price options on products they sell or source.
  - Waitrose supermarkets in the UK: promote quality and service over price, and enjoy consistent growth & good profits
  - Stella Artois was always promoted as 'reassuringly expensive' in the UK during the 1990s, where it became the No 1 premium lager by a huge margin. (Incidentally, this was undermined when the owners started doing discount price deals on it in supermarkets, and promptly removed the USP!)
- A curious, but real, economic fact: the more you pay for something, then the more it's worth. For example: in my profession, if I give material away, people rarely pay attention to it … but if I charge a fair price, then it usually has a good effect!
- And always remember: reducing your price won't affect your 'customer experience' one bit!

The long term

For long term success we need to consider that being 'great', (and consistently evolving and improving … because what is 'great' today is 'commonplace' tomorrow), will be the only way to deliver long term profit and success.

This is a marathon not a sprint.

There is no longer any such thing as a 'job for life' – skills are changing so quickly that skills you have today may be redundant tomorrow.

The old industrial/advertising model is now starting to die. Businesses can no longer rely on large sales and marketing budgets to drive sales – the customer is king!

Consistently delivering outstanding customer experiences, is the ONLY sensible long term success strategy for any organisation. Sure, if you just want a 'short term hit' go for short term profit above everything else and get out quick, but, in all other circumstances, work on delivering excellent customer experiences, as well as short term profit ... it must be a sensible and healthy balance!

Immortality

I always find it amusing how much money is spent on cosmetics, and anti-wrinkle creams to help you look younger, all this stuff that costs a fortune and all it does in reality is change appearances.

Appearances are only skin deep.

Actually *the only way to achieve immortality is to be great at what you do*.

- If you are a waiter, it makes sense to try and be the best waiter in town.
- If you are a salesman, it makes sense to try and be the best salesman you can be
- If you are a business owner, it makes sense to try and make your business as great as possible (which is not the same as 'as large as possible')
- If you are a manager, it makes sense to try and be the best manager you can be (and wouldn't we like to know what people really think of us as managers ... are we 'great', or are we 'a bit of a prat' ... because there's not a lot in between the two!)

Conversely, it makes no sense whatever to not try and do these things.

Being 'great' in whatever you do is rewarding, fun and energising. And, if you feel disempowered, remember the following quote from Mother Teresa:

'In life, we cannot do great things, we can only do small things with great love.'

To conclude, I'd ask you to consider this:

- If you don't know why you should bother to 'be great' or not, then think: *'what would I want someone to say at my funeral?'*
    - Would it be, 'gosh we'll really miss them, they were so good, they were such a pleasure to be around, and they've achieved these great things?'
    - Or would it be, 'thank god that's over, what's for lunch?'

It's your choice, whatever you do with your life will determine what people will say about you. You could even suggest that the answer to this question is effectively your own personal definition of 'success'!

... and if you're thinking 'I don't care what someone will say at my funeral as I'll be dead', just remember: the whole purpose of considering this question at all is to help guide you to make effective choices while you're alive ... don't miss the point!

If you're not sure, think about it, discuss it with people you trust, and come up with an answer.

If you do have an answer, and it's not pointing to an overwhelming desire to be 'great', then I suggest you either change your attitude (before your competition do it for you), or get out of what you are doing now and do something that you are more motivated by.

Back to business

In the business world, *sales and marketing budgets* can sometimes be the same as 'anti-wrinkle cream' – they are often driven by external appearance only, and try to influence people to buy in order to *drive sales for the short-term*. In order to keep this up for the long-term, the sales and marketing budgets need to be continually increased and developed.

Not a very sensible or profitable way to do business for either the company or the customer.

(Remember: your competition is always looking for ways to put you out of business. If you are spending money unnecessarily on sales and marketing, this is a cost to your business that can be cut out and the savings passed on to the customer. Your competitors will know how to do this, and, if you don't pull your finger out and look at this realistically, the first thing you will know about it is when this has already happened).

This is not a new problem.

'Customer service' is an old chestnut and it doesn't seem to be getting any better, as a customer we experience frustration.

- Trains are late with no explanation,
- there are queues at shops and banks with people milling about behind the counter not helping,
- there are politicians who are only interested in getting re elected (or the size of their expenses)
- there are disinterested waiters and waitresses who then have the cheek to ask you if 'everything is OK with your meal', and of course you always say it's 'fine',
- and then there's the accountant and the solicitor who is only interested in the size of the bill rather than whether they have delivered what you actually wanted in the first place.

It's completely dysfunctional and in our jobs, we can often feel like we are trying to 'wade through mud'. The same mistakes happen over and over again, complaints happen that should never have arisen, and we spend a fortune trying to resolve them, customers leave us without any thanks and don't even tell us, follow ups to sales don't happen and we miss out on massive opportunities.

I could go on forever, but these are all caused by systemic issues in your beliefs and your organisation that you are working for and they are all solvable.

2

SOME FACTS

What I'd like you to feel after reading this book are three things.

1. You understand the issues
2. You feel motivated and empowered to do something about the issues
3. You know what action to take

If you take one action from this book then it is worth your while having read it, if you do nothing then all I have done is waste your time. Don't waste your time – it's annoying and frustrating!

Here are some facts that will give you some real hard data about this 'customer service' subject. Because this is a bit of a 'soft' problem.

People think, 'well it's just "customer service", it doesn't really make that much difference. HR or "customer service" will take care of that ...' Instinctively we actually know that it does really matter, but we find it very hard to find some facts that prove it,

So here they are.

1. When we get great service from a business we tell a few people in a short space of time. But when we get bad service we tend to tell as many people as possible. **Bad news travels at least ten times as fast as good news.** Just watch the news on your TV if you want proof of this!
2. **It is <u>at least</u> 6 times as expensive to get a new customer as it is to look after an existing one.** I find this a particularly interesting one because so many businesses have massive sales and marketing budgets, but then baulk at training their people or putting a budget in place for 'existing customers'. A budget for customer service will be 6 times as effective, at least,

as anything the organisation spends on sales and marketing to attract new customers! Indeed I have worked with one business where it was almost 200 times as effective to do this. So it can be massive. A simple and frequent example of poor practice in this area can be seen in Insurance Companies and Banks who spend a fortune luring new customers to 'change to them', but when they've got you, you're just treated as 'one of the herd'.

3. **60–70% of customer defections are because of 'perceived indifference'** from the organisation, rather than actual 'bad service'. So it's critically important to get all this right – no one is trying to be 'indifferent', it's just that we're always so busy every day that things simply don't get done as attentively and proactively as we might like them to be. This is perceived by the customer as 'indifference'.

4. **Increasing customer loyalty by 1% can have the same effect on the bottom line of your business as decreasing costs by up to 10%.** I guess this is hugely important as we are always looking to decrease costs in business, but just consider it's probably 10 times as effective to increase customer loyalty as it is to cut costs. So finance directors and accountants please remember this! Anyone can cut costs, it's easy to do because we can see it, it's a 'present' measure. You just have to have the belief that building customer loyalty will pay off on the bottom line over the long term if it's done properly (what we call a 'future success measure')

5. **If you get it wrong, the vast majority of your customers won't tell you** – who'll they tell instead?

6. The big one! **80% of your customers will leave your business saying they are 'satisfied' with the service or products that you have given them.** That's 4 out of 5 people who are 'satisfied' but who will still leave. These are the people who are 'indifferent' to you, because you're just 'OK', and not 'great'. In fact, as stated above, a recent survey measured that the number one reason for customer defection (by a large margin) was 'perceived indifference'. [This survey stated that 63% of defections were due to this reason, as opposed to product

or service dissatisfaction ... which was only 14%]. Of course, all this information is common sense, and we could state a plethora of reports and as many different stats as you like. The point is very clear: **customer loyalty is driven not by product or service but by the emotion that product or service evokes in the customer** – and customers want more than 'OK' ... they want 'great'.

So we have to conclude that

> **'Satisfied' customers are not enough. You are either 'great' or 'poor'.**

Now all this is becoming even more important these days because the single most powerful influencer of success, motivator of people and sales building machine ... 'word of mouth' ... is spreading at the speed of light via the internet.

In the old days you could tell your friends, you could tell your network and you could tell your community, and news would travel quite quickly. A good example of that would be Ratners, the jewellers, who, after an infamous speech by its chairman, went from being the most profitable jewellery business in the world to bankrupt in under a year.

But now *word of mouth can spread at the speed of light*, through social networking, specialist feedback sites and the like.

So 'customer experience' is becoming more and more important, and the figures I have just discussed will just get more and more extreme. (And please note: the 'feedback' part of the internet, is still really in it's infancy, it's not working well yet, but it will because that's where the demand is).

A good example of this: a short while ago I received an email from Trip Advisor which told me about the dirtiest hotels of 2011 on the front page. Well of course I'm going to click on that and I'm going to look at those hotels, and my bet will be that those hotels will be out of business by the end of the year.

So again, as the facts clearly show: **you are either 'great' or 'poor'.**

3

MAKING IT WORK

So, on a daily basis how does this work? I think it's fair to say that most people would agree with these statements:

- We all have too much to do every day.
- Things don't always happen like we'd want them to.
- We often spend too much time on unimportant things.
- Not everyone in our organisation is 100% motivated and empowered.
- Sometimes we don't know exactly what the word on the street is about our business, and we're a bit worried about it.

What I am going to tell you now will enable you to:

- Spend less time on the unimportant things,
- spend more time on the important stuff,
- make sure that things happen as planned,
- give great customer service as normal,
- have motivated and empowered people, and
- know what the word on the street is and know what to do to make it great.

But first, here's another question,

Why are we all in business?

Now I bet you said something like, 'to make money', and you'd be right.

It is always the answer I get when I ask this question at open seminars, and the question I then ask is:

How do we do that?

Because if we are in business just to 'make money', we may well make some howling mistakes to 'make money' today, that will destroy 'making money' tomorrow.

So you have to conclude, that *money is important, but we are not in business solely to make money.*

We are in fact in business to deliver an experience to the customer that is so good that people want to pay us for it. This is so important I am going to repeat it – we are not in business to make money,

We are in business to deliver an experience that is so good that people <u>want</u> to pay us for it.

So, how do we get this service that is so good?
Service is actually just

'actions we take' .

Actions we take determine the

'results that we get'.

If we want to get better or different results, we have to

'take different actions'.

Another statement of common sense!
But what influences the action we take?

The answer to that is that our ***beliefs and emotions influence the actions we take.***

We all want quick results ... and this desire will drive our actions through our beliefs and emotions.

So, if we believe we are in business to make money we will take actions that will make us money today.

Which are, unfortunately, often at the expense of making money tomorrow.

For example:

- We will get our calls answered by a machine rather than by a person because it is more profitable.
- We will have a credit control department that will stop orders in the last week of the month to reduce overdues.
- We will not trust our staff with a budget to deal with any customer issues – anything that requires expenditure will need to be authorised by a manager
- We will do sales calls out of hours from a call centre abroad because it's cheaper to do it that way.

- We will not spend money on training that doesn't have an immediate effect, or isn't a statutory requirement
- We'll not follow up service queries because we haven't got the time.
- We'll make it hard for customers to complain or get their money back.
- We'll not do any systematic customer surveying because it's too expensive and might create problems for us *[Note: from experience it creates many times more opportunities than problems ... many times!]*
- We will reduce staff numbers to make bottom line budget at the end of the year.
- We'll have special offers that are hidden old stock clearance deals.
- We will give great offers for new customers but baulk at giving value away to existing customers to build loyalty
- We will chase butterflies while the elephants are escaping...

These actions are driven by the belief that we are in business solely 'to make money'.

It's great to spell them out, because it's so obvious how silly, disempowering and value destroying this narrow mindset can be.

Now if we believe we are in business 'to deliver a customer experience that is so good that people want to pay us for it'

- we wouldn't have our calls answered by a machine, we wouldn't stop our orders the last week of the month, we would trust our staff with budgets to resolve issues and take proactive actions, we wouldn't prospect call people at horrible times, we'd train people persistently and excellently, we'd follow up all our service queries, we'd make it easy for customers to complain / feedback / return goods, we systematically survey all our customers in a customer friendly way (very important), we'd ring fence all expenditure that delivers the 'customer experience' and look for savings elsewhere, we'd treat existing customers as well as (or better than) new ones, and we'd be honest about all our offers.

The great examples of people doing this well can be seen in the successful supermarket chains across the world. In the UK Tesco powered ahead of it's rivals by focusing on customer needs excellently (as well as controlling costs and having some great marketing!)

So why doesn't it happen, what is the real issue, what goes wrong?

I often hear the following reasons: we don't have the time to do all that stuff, communication is poor, the systems don't work, we've all got too much to do, we're doing OK at the moment, my manager's got a poor attitude so I just don't do it, people are lazy, I'm not paid enough, no one's trained me, and it goes on and on and on.

We've got to break this vicious circle, we have to throw it in reverse and call it a virtuous circle that drives forward great performance.

Some examples

Here are three examples of businesses where great service does happen, where they know they are in business 'to deliver a customer experience that is so good that people want to pay for it' and they should serve as positive examples to help you understand this point.

Example 1: Enterprise Rent a Car

Enterprise Rent a Car have grown from being a small business in the 1960's to being the largest car rental business in the west.

How did they do this? By **obsessive focus on customers as their first priority.**

An example of this would be when they were entering the insurance market, (when you have a prang in your car you need a hire car, which you will get from a car rental company).

Enterprise were providing hire cars to people but were finding that the service they were giving was not very good, because they were part of a larger system, with four parties in the loop, that, by its nature, could not deliver a great customer experience.

The four parties in the loop were: the insurance company, the owner of the car, the garage who was repairing the car and the car rental company.

The service that was being given to the person who rented the car was poor because there was poor communication, changed timescales, and lots of chasing around for all parties.

Enterprise know they are not in business to make money, they are in business 'to deliver a customer experience that is so good that people want to pay them'. So they said to themselves:

'We don't do 'poor' experiences, we only do 'great''

So they looked into it by commissioning a survey that asked, 'what do we need to do to resolve this?'

What they found they needed to do to resolve this was to put a multi-million dollar computer system in place to bring all these people together. If they did this, not only would it cost them millions of dollars to put the system in place, but also it would reduce the average rental times by up to a day (so, in the short term, it's a very expensive decision!).

So if you're the finance director (who may be in business to 'make money') what are you going to say?

You're going to say,

'No, don't do this it's not going to make us any money, it's a stupid thing to do!'.

What did Enterprise actually do?

Well, of course you guessed it, they did it.

What then happened?

Well, in the first year they made less money – but what happened in the second, and all subsequent years?

The Insurance companies saw Enterprise as the easiest business to deal with in the market, and one that gave them and their (the insurance companies') customers a consistently excellent experience, and their insurance business sky rocketed.

The rest is history.

For more detailed information on this story please see *Exceeding Customer Expectations: What Enterprise, America's #1 Car Rental Company, Can Teach You about Creating Lifetime Customers* by Kirk Kazanjian.

Example 2: Merck Pharmaceuticals

Merck Pharmaceuticals has a mission statement that goes like this:

> ***Our business is preserving and improving human life*** *… All of our actions must be measured by our success in achieving these goals. We value, above all, our ability to serve everyone who can benefit from the appropriate use of our products and services, thereby providing lasting consumer satisfaction.*
> *(http://www.merck.com/about/our-values/home.html?WT. svl=mainnav)*

Very similar to what I have just been saying to you.

While they were researching, they developed a drug that treated a disease called River Blindness. River Blindness affects people in a part of the world who are generally poor and cannot afford medicines.

So what are Merck going to do?

They've developed a drug for this disease, it cost them a fortune developing it and it's going to cost them a fortune to manufacture and distribute it. But the people that need it can't afford it, what are they going to do?

Well, your finance director (who is in business to 'make money') would say: 'Don't do it, it wont make money!'. And he or she would be right.

But Merck think, 'Our business is preserving & improving human life'. They develop it and distribute it free as part of a charity foundation.

The benefit of that is, when you are trying to do business with Merck are you likely to trust them? The answer of course is yes, if they can stick to their principles in a situation like that, they are going to stick by their principles in any situation. They are a company to be trusted and to do business with.

For more information on this, please see *http://www.merck.com/ responsibility/access/access-feature-mectizan.html.*

Example 3: Marks and Spencer

The third example is a simple and recent example in the UK.

Department store 'Marks and Spencer' were caught out by the press for charging £1 more for larger sizes of bras than for smaller sizes. This caused an outrage in the press.

The very next day M&S put a full page advert in all the main papers with a picture of their bra and it said quite clearly underneath it, 'we boobed'.

Photo reproduced by kind permission on Marks & Spencer Plc, Uli Weber (www. uliweber.com) and Natalie Suliman

Now can you trust a business like that? Of course you can, because if they're going to be honest when they've made a mistake, spend a lot of money publicising and rectifying it, then they're going to be honest when times are good as well.

So why doesn't this common sense stuff happen, what goes wrong? Why isn't it common practice? In order to answer that question we have to first of all understand how organisations work.

The Operational Effectiveness Cycle

Every organisations has this cycle, from one-man-bands to huge multi-national companies.

First of all there is a group of people called 'stakeholders', these are owners, employees, suppliers, the community they are in fact, everyone who is affected by this business.

These stakeholders, whether they know it or not, have something called a 'vision', (this is a belief – a reason for being a stakeholder, a reason for doing what we do).

This vision turns into what's called a 'mission'.

The 'mission' produces 'strategy', 'strategy' produces 'processes', 'processes' produce 'behaviour' and 'behaviour' gives 'results'.

Now when we're talking about 'customer service' where do we generally focus?

The answer of course is 'behaviour' and 'processes'.

But we know that behaviour and processes are only a result of strategy and mission, vision and stakeholders.

So the root of all customer experiences is vision, mission and strategy.

Followed by systems and processes.

Getting it wrong at this level produces a huge lack of trust, a lack of trust with the customer, and really importantly a lack of trust within the organisation. So as people go for short term profit at the expense of giving a great service, it causes frustration, aggravation, poor behaviour and therefore poor results.

So, usually, the single most important reason as to why this common sense isn't common practice in organisations is because of one of the following reasons:

- The organisational effectiveness chart hasn't been thought through with the overriding desire to 'give great customer experiences', under the belief system that 'we are in business to give such great customer experiences that people want to pay us for them'.
- It's been thought through with some other overriding desire. (This shows up to everyone else as a 'hidden agenda' – and customers and employees HATE this!)
- It is very often only considered from the point of view of efficiency towards making money in the present ... incredibly shortsighted!

Here are some important questions that you may want to ask about your organisation:

- **Stakeholders:** how can the people deliver 'great customer experiences' when the stakeholders are only interested in money?
- **Vision:** how can the people deliver 'great customer experiences' when the vision and belief system is self-centred and focused entirely on enriching the owner stakeholders and senior management?
- **Mission:** how can the people deliver 'great customer experiences' when there is no clear mission that will guide them through the hard times and ensure they stick to this belief no matter what?
- **Strategy:** how can the people deliver 'great customer experiences' when the strategy is focused on cost reduction and cutting out 'unnecessary' expense that adds value to the customer?
- **Processes:** how can the people deliver 'great customer experiences' when the processes are 'company focused' rather than 'customer-focused' (i.e. they suit the company's need for efficiency rather than the customer's need for a great experience)?
- **Behaviour:** how can the people deliver 'great customer experiences' when their behaviour is constantly monitored and criticised without all of the above issues being resolved effectively?
- **Remember:** you can take a horse to water, but you can't make it drink.
- **Results:** how can the people deliver 'great customer experiences' when the only results that are measured are all focused on the short term financial numbers?
- And, very importantly, **leading by example:** how can the people deliver 'great customer experiences' when everyone, at all levels, does not lead this by example?

Every organisation, team, and individual must consider these questions carefully, examine their own belief systems, and ask themselves if they have what it takes to stick by common sense even when it conflicts with short-term profit.

Because, if you cannot stick by this when times are bad, you cannot stick with it at all.

- Your people will be disengaged at best, and actively looking for other employment at worst.
- Your customers will be disengaged at best, and actively looking for other suppliers at worst.

The Upside Down Triangle

Another huge reason why this common sense isn't common practice, and organisations are unable to deliver consistently excellent customer experiences, is down to the way they organise themselves.

When I go into a organisation, I ask them, 'please can I have a copy of your organisational structure' and they hand me a piece of paper with something on it that looks a bit like a triangle ... who is at the top and who is at the bottom?

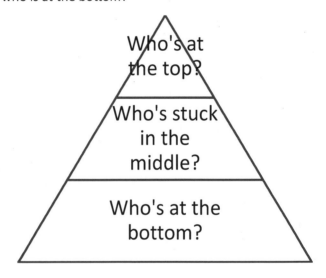

And where are the customers?

Well, who is at the top? The head-honcho is at the top, the MD, the chairman, all at the top. Who is at the bottom? All the people who are customer facing.

Where are the customers on this chart? Customers are off the diagram at the bottom!

Now what does this say?

A picture speaks a thousand words

What it says is, that the person at the top is more important than the people at the bottom, the management are more important than the customers.

So when someone who is customer facing is dealing with a problem with a customer, or even an opportunity with a customer, the customer wants one thing and the management say they should do another. What are they going to do?

Well of course they know who pays their wages (directly) (and, of course, they have forgotten who really pays those wages). Customer service goes out the window, and everyone does what their boss tells them to do, whether it's going to produce customer loyalty and great customer experiences, or not.

A recipe for disaster.

So if you are really serious about making some changes, the first thing to do is to **turn this triangle upside down**, and publish it to everyone in your business and tell them what you have done and why.

The customer *really is* King!

By the way, taking this action has other huge benefits:

Management's role now changes from 'command and control' (this is called the industrial age mindset ... see below), to 'direct and support'. Unfortunately, people who have spent their whole lives getting to the top of the triangle sometimes don't feel too happy about being told this news!

'The people at the sharp end' now have a totally different role as well: rather than perhaps being disempowered victims who can only complain about all the issues they experience but feel they can do nothing about, they now need to be empowered and proactive, not only to make sure the customer actually receives an outstanding experience, but also to ensure that the management are kept informed about what they can do to help them consistently deliver this ongoing!

Industrial age mindset

The 'industrial age mindset' is what produced 'command and control' thinking.

The industrial age valued machinery and capital investment backed up by marketing and distribution systems, above all else, as a way of creating wealth – and this has worked very well.

In order to make this work, the manager's role was to 'command and control'. People were expected just to turn up and do their job ... little thinking was required!

But we are now in a new age – *the 21st-century is the 'knowledge age'*. In order to get the best out of people today they must be empowered and motivated. *This cannot happen with an 'industrial age mindset'.*

How often are people today asked to deliver more for less?

And how often are these people working in organisations that suffer from the 'industrial age mindset' where they are not valued, not empowered, and indeed completely restricted by strategy, systems, and processes that will in fact get in the way of them delivering this outstanding customer experience that is critical for success in today's market.

I have even worked with an organisation where the 'managers' were not allowed to 'manage' their people, only the systems. In order to take any 'management' actions with regards their people, they had first of all to get permission from head office!

This outdated and ineffective mindset is unfortunately prevalent in the western countries that did so well out of the Industrial Revolution. And they are, unfortunately, supported by:

Industrial age accounting policies

The accounting policies we use today are based on the 'industrial age mindset' which values machines as an 'investment' and people as a 'cost'.

Now what do businesses always want to do?

They want to make investments and reduce costs.

So what are they going to do with their people? They're not going to train them (it's a 'cost'), they're going to pay them the minimum they can get away with (it's a 'cost') and they're going to invest their money in machines, and of course customer service goes out the window!

And what figures do your accounts measure?

Figures that are history! These are important for judging certain things and perhaps predicting future figures (although they're usually far too slowly produced to be of any REAL help), but if you only have these figures in this business, it's like trying to drive your car using only the rear view mirror ...

... another recipe for disaster.

So some real changes are needed!

(And one of the greatest changes I strongly recommend is putting some much more effective measures into your business – ones that predict 'future success' rather than only having ones that show 'past or present (at best) success'. More information on this will be given in Chapter 9 : 'Measure').

Every organisation sees itself from the inside out

Another reason why great customer experiences aren't common practice is that every organisation will see itself from the inside out.

It's incredible, as a customer, how perceptive you can be about someone else's business, you can see exactly where things are going wrong, from simple interactions (such as sitting in a café where the staff are sitting chatting while tables remain uncleared).

But if you then join that business as an employee, that perception dies over night, because from that moment you see yourself from the inside out.

But ***the customer is always seeing you from the outside in.***

So businesses very often will get all their internal systems and processes all organised and efficient to make sure they're not wasting resources. But the one thing they don't do is get that last bit organised, outside from their point of view, which coincidentally is the first bit the customer sees of you, and from the customer's point of view it is called a 'moment of truth'.

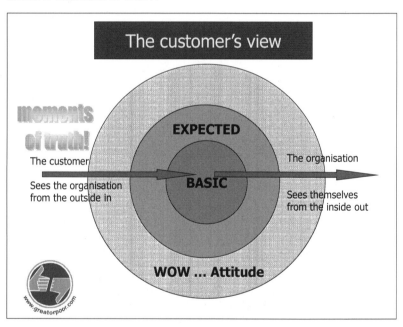

The term 'moment of truth' is a very important term, because it means it is 'true' for your customer. If it's true then they'll tell everyone about it. (And remember: which are they likely to focus on more ... the good things or the bad ones?)

Now if you organise your moments of truth, you think about each one systematically in turn, and you make sure you have systems and processes in place to make sure they are excellent, the customer will talk about those. If you don't organise them, you'll rely on 'common sense' and they'll be left up to chance, and chance is not a kind master when you need to deliver excellence as standard.

ALL your 'moments of truth' have to be organised. You have to have a system in place to recognise them and deal with them – you can never anticipate all of them, but you can continually pick them up and manage them to continually improve...

For example:

- a queue in a shop: do you have a specific policy on how to organise queues, take action to reduce them, make sure that the customer has a good experience when they are in them ... or do you just leave it to chance?
- how long a phone takes to answer: do you have a specific policy on how to ensure the customer gets a great experience on the phone whether there are queues or not ... or do you just put on hold music in place and hope for the best?
- whether someone says hello to you as soon as you walk through the door in a restaurant or not: have you trained people on this and do you use it as a key performance measurement ... or do you just leave it to chance and hope that your people will use some common sense?

If you don't organise it, it probably won't happen ... and your moments of truth will turn into moments of nightmare more often than not for your customer.

Which they will spread to the world at the speed of light!

Simple, simple, simple things that make huge differences to businesses. Because, to a customer...

...actions speak louder than words.

(Here's some good news: as you read on, you'll find that the 'Great or Poor' system will give you all the tools you need to continually evaluate, improve and monitor your moments of truth – you cannot possibly look at them all in one go, but perhaps you could improve 1 every week?)

The basic human need for attention

There is a basic human need for attention ... just ask anyone with young children. When a child comes home from school they want attention more than anything else. We never lose this need, but we do start to hide it as we grow up ... but, as customers, this need is the single most powerful influencer of our 'experience'.

This need has no warning signs (unlike hunger for example), but it is as basic a need as the need for food and water. We are social animals.

But, so often we're busy 'doing our jobs', that we forget about this need – we just 'don't have time' in our quest for efficiency. But, no matter whether you have time or not, your customer still has this need: *they want your attention just as if they were your children.*

Isn't it ironic that so often we find it easier to deliver this automatically via the Internet than we do in person ... I have a great relationship with Amazon.com, I feel they are very attentive to my needs, and yet I've never ever interacted with a human in their organisation!

Customers will demand attention no matter what. And how is this repaid by them? As previously covered:

- if you're 'great' they'll remain loyal and promote you
- if you're 'OK' they'll drift away because you've not fulfilled this need
- if you're 'poor' they'll resent you and try to harm you

It's as simple as that!

Summary

What stops the obvious common sense of great customer service from being common practice on a daily basis?

- The Mission not having been thought through, throughout the whole organisation. (What are we in business to do?)
- Having a 'Money focused mission'.
- The Mission not being applied to everything.
- Lack of staff involvement / engagement with the Mission.
- Strategy, procedure, systems and behaviour not aligned with a 'Customer-Focused Mission' (more later).
- Industrial age accounting policies.
- Upside down company organisational charts.
- Lack of attention to 'moments of truth'.
- Not realising what the customer's REAL needs are
- Almost everything ... if it's not aligned to the Customer-Focused Mission.
- Not having systems and processes that continually 'Go the Extra Inch'
- And last, but not least, no effective measurement of service!

In other words: it's lots of things, that are prevalent in many organisations.

And most organisations don't have a system to address this!

Oh dear!

But, don't despair, help is at hand. In order to deliver outstanding customer experiences consistently and effectively, you need systems that obsessively make this happen.

As Ray Kroc, the architect of McDonald's amazing success, famously said:

'If you want extraordinary results from ordinary people, you need extraordinary systems.'

Below, you will find the greatorpoor system that, if applied properly, will definitely result in a huge improvement and consistent development of your customer experience – resulting, in turn, in increased sales and profits, combined with reduced costs.

4

GOLDEN EGGS

The goose that laid the golden egg

You may recall from your childhood the story of 'the goose that laid a golden egg'.

In this story a poor farmer owns a goose which one day lays a golden egg. The farmer's delighted, he looks after this wonderful goose and it continues to lay golden eggs for him. Until one day the farmer, who has become fabulously wealthy, becomes greedy and now one egg per day is no longer good enough.

He has expensive habits and commitments.

So he cuts down on goose expenses, stops looking after the goose so well and eventually his basic instincts get the better of him and he chops off the head of the goose because he wants all of the golden eggs now, only to find that there are none inside.

So it is with organisations:

- the goose is your organisation and your stakeholders,
- the golden eggs are the profits,

Obviously one has to look after, cherish and nurture the goose in order for it to continue to thrive and lay more and more golden eggs, and usually it's really easy to look after the goose when she's laying golden eggs, (but beware the senior managers who demand more and more golden eggs every year, but are not prepared to invest in the health and welfare of the goose!)

The question people need to search their souls for and ask all their stakeholders to agree with is:

- do we have the courage and determination to stick by the goose, keep feeding and looking after her, when she goes through a barren patch and the eggs are temporarily less plentiful or will we, like so many organisations, especially those who answer to short term shareholders above all else, cut down on her feed and welfare or even lop her pretty head off and reach inside only to find there's nothing for the long term?

Very often the smallest things choke us up in an organisation and usually, from the customer's point of view, very often *the small things are the big things.*

As customers we don't care if a company's the cheapest if they are painful to deal with.

We don't care if a company's the fastest if they're not accurate.

We don't care if they're the most innovative if they're not caring in every little detail of every transaction, every day.

Every organisation must look after their goose carefully, obsessively and lovingly. Prioritise her needs above yours and she will continue to lay golden eggs.

And remember, it's quite easy to understand that you need to improve the lot of your goose when she is laying sporadically, but it takes an obsessive genius to continue to develop and prioritise this care and attention when the eggs come every day. (And how many organisations have made this mistake!)

But you have to because if you neglect any part of this, the eggs will stop coming over time.

So what's the answer? We've laid our foundations, it's now time to build the house.

5

THE GREAT OR POOR SYSTEM

The answer is a simple 4-step process starting with

'our beliefs and emotions'

and proceeding via

'our actions'

through to

'how we measure them, follow them up and make sure they keep improving' (our results)

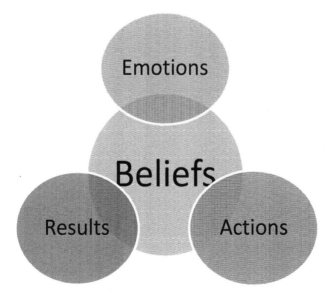

You will see the four step process below. It looks a bit like a fly-wheel. It is designed in this way to represent a fly-wheel at the heart of your organisation, driving excellence and ongoing improvement via systems ... no matter who's in charge or whatever else is happening. **This is a fly-wheel to drive your organisation forward.**

You'll see at the centre something called 'CFM', this stands for 'Customer-Focused Mission' (this represents our 'beliefs').

What this means is that every organisation needs to have at the core of their whole organisation the sincere and obsessive belief that **'we are in business to deliver experiences that are so good that people want to pay us for them'**. This can be expressed in many ways, but needs to be at the heart of any organisation that wants to excel – without this sincere and passionate belief, long term success is nigh on impossible.

Moving up from that it says, **'find the customers REAL needs'**, (this is all about emotions). We mentioned this right at the beginning: customers actually just want you to care and pay attention to them. This principle is all about basic human psychology and knowing what drives consumer behaviour.

The third point is **'go the extra inch'**, (This is about actions). Now so often we hear people saying, 'go the extra mile', but we researched this point doggedly and would have to do disagree vehemently. The 'extra mile' is unsustainable, annoying, demotivating and frustrating. One of my goals in life is to see the phrase 'go the extra mile' erased from the vocabulary of customer service (and the other phrase I want to see the back of is 'customer satisfaction')!

When I say to people: 'how do you feel when your boss or your organisation asks you to go the extra mile?' The answer always is, 'it's too far, it's too difficult and it's unsustainable'.

On top of this and, most importantly, it's likely to be inconsistent (and the one thing customers really crave is consistency) – if you deliver an extra mile today, the customer will expect at least an extra mile tomorrow (and preferably two!).

So I say: 'could you go the extra inch?'

'Well yes we could.'

'Could you do it in everything that you do?'

'Yes we could.'

'Would you find it empowering if your organisation enabled and encouraged you to go an extra inch all the time?'

'Yes we would.'

'And if you moved an inch forward in everything, regularly and systematically, would that produce significant progress over time?'

'Yes of course it would.'

So it's **go the extra inch**, not the extra mile, because we can do it and it's empowering, energising, and relatively easy ... but we can't do the extra mile.

The last point you will see on the diagram says 'measure'. (This is about results!)

Why would we want to measure this? ***Many customer surveys and measures are pointless.*** They don't work at best, and they destroy customer service at worst!

But we have to have a measure – because what gets measured gets done. We have to know what the results are at any point in time. How well would a football team play if there was no clear score, or they didn't know what position they were in the league? They'd just 'kick the ball around', and, of course, this is exactly what many people do at work on a daily basis!

The measurement I am proposing is very simple and very powerful

It is absolutely vital to measure the customer experience for three reasons.

1. **It's the root of long term success.**
2. **What gets measured gets done.**
3. **If we can measure something we can move it forward.**

So here's more information on the four principles of great or poor.

6

CUSTOMER-FOCUSED MISSION

Lets start by looking at the Customer-Focused Mission. This is all about beliefs.

'The true motivator for employees is the spirit of cooperation that comes with a shared vision.'
Richard Denny

Customer-Focused Mission

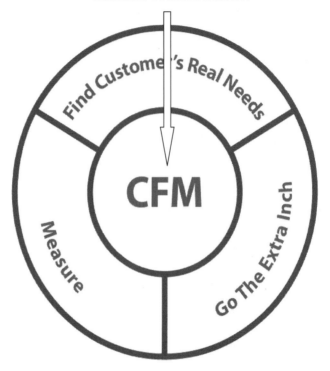

What I would like you to imagine is that you're in a jungle, you're hacking your way through and you're trying to get to a destination. Now, how useful would a map be? I think the answer would be: not very useful.

What you need, when you are in a jungle, is a compass. I think it's fair to say that business, and indeed life, today is a lot more like hacking through a jungle than following a map. We all need a compass to see us on our way and we all need to know which direction to go in.

The 'customer-focused mission' is your compass.

And, of course, your compass needs to be at the centre of your organisation, so it influences and guides everything you do. This is not a 'balanced scorecard' – your CFM should be the centre of EVERYTHING.

Now, the direction comes from the 'vision'.
  The vision means:

- Why are we doing this, what is our purpose here on earth and why do we want to do these sorts of things?

Then the mission stems from this and asks the question:

- What do we need to do, from the customers' point of view … in order to fulfil our vision?

This can be a very difficult balance. Let's help you get to grips with this.

Vision

In order to look at your vision, you need to ask yourself two questions.

1. **Why am I doing this?**
2. **What do I want to be famous for?**

So lets look at those in turn.

Firstly, **why am I doing <u>this</u>?** You have to ask yourself this specific question, with the emphasis on the word 'this' – but it seems to me to be the one question people never ask themselves.

Very often I get the answer, well because it's nine o'clock on Monday morning.

That isn't good enough – if you haven't got an inner drive or strong motivation in your life (or at least in what you're doing in your job or career), then life is just a 'waiting room' ... and waiting rooms are not known for being exciting and inspiring, fulfilling places!

In order to deliver greatness in your life you have to ask yourself, why am I doing **<u>THIS</u>**? It might be a stepping stone to something else, but be sure you know why you are doing it.

Because just paying your mortgage, just getting by, will never produce greatness ... on the contrary it will produce a lose/lose result:

*   You will lose because you will be spending a significant portion of your life doing something that doesn't fulfil you
*   Your organisation will lose because they will not be getting a great performance out of you
*   The customer will lose because they will be getting a much poorer experience than they could do (and isn't this so often the case?)

Question two: **what do I want to be famous for?**

This links, obviously, to the first question. Because we're all famous for something, whether we like it or not – and frankly there's not a lot of gap between, 'they're a fantastic person', and, 'they're a bit of a prat'.

From an organisational point of view there's not a lot of gap between 'they're fantastic', and 'they're not bad'.

You will definitely always be famous for something – remember, it's called 'the word on the street'.

So let's put some real thought into this and make sure we're famous for things that we choose, and not famous for things that we don't choose … by default!

It's absolutely vital to get this right, so please stop and consider these questions now.

When you've spent some time on this and you've got some helpful answers, then you need to ask yourself:

- **'What is my mission ... my Customer-Focused Mission?'**

Firstly, who is my customer?
The answer to that is, *everybody you deal with.*

Everybody is your customer

- Paying customers are the customers of everybody
- Employees are the customers of managers (who is it indeed who hires people and physically pays the wages?)
- Managers are the customers of employees (who is it indeed who enables you to get your job done properly and therefore be paid?)
- and so it goes on and on and on

There are customers who pay us money and customers who don't. But the point being is the customer is everyone.

(So this is good news at it means you can apply these principles to every area of your life!)

So, whatever your mission is, it has to relate to your relationships with everyone.

The question you ask yourself is this, 'if there were no barriers, what would I want these customers to say about me behind my back?'

They're already saying things behind your back – so you might as well make it as good as possible ... or even great!

- What would I WANT my paying customers to say about me?
- What would I WANT my boss to say about me?
- What would I WANT my employees to say about me?
- What would I WANT my colleagues to say about me?
- What would I WANT my family to say about me?
- Etc etc etc

From an organisational point of view:

- What would we WANT our paying customers to say about us?
- What would we WANT our investors to say about us?
- What would we WANT our employees to say about us?
- What would we WANT our suppliers to say about us?
- What would we WANT our community to say about us?
- Etc etc etc

People talk about other people and about organisations as a whole. The question is, what do you want them to say? Rather than what are they actually saying?

Some people who have thought this through in the UK are Carlsberg.

Carlsberg have great adverts. I particularly like the one below.

The point being, 'Carlsberg don't do taxis, but if they did they would be the best in the world'.

Those of you who are familiar with those adverts know what I'm talking about. It's called thinking outside the box. It's thinking: 'if there were no barriers what would I really want my customers to say behind my back?'

What a great example – so let's all try and **start thinking differently.**

And then, of course you have to start applying the same questions and thinking to your:

- Group
- Team
- Department
- Organisation

This principle not only applies to all customers, it also applies at all levels in an organisation. Every level should have a clear and empowering CFM ... and they all need to align with each other!

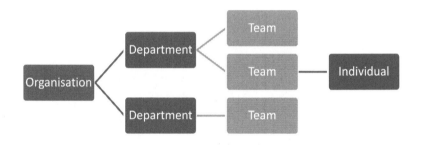

So how important is this? Well, here are a couple of examples.

Example number one is a supermarket based in the UK, called Tesco.

Their core purpose is **to create value for customers to earn their lifetime loyalty.**

I would call this their 'vision'.

Tesco have what I would call a 'customer-focused mission' stemming from this (using my words, not theirs) and anyone who has been to a Tesco will know it. It's very simple and it's only three words, and it goes like this:

'Every little helps'.

What that means is:

- when I'm stacking shelves at Tesco ... every little helps,
- when a customer is asking me for directions to where the yoghurts are ... every little helps,
- when there's a queue at the checkout ... every little helps,
- when I'm negotiating with a buyer ... every little helps.

It's hugely important, it's completely empowering and absolutely critical to the success of that organisation.

For more information, please see *http://www.tescoplc.com/plc/about_us/values/*

The second example I would like to mention is Disney. Now Disney's customer-focused mission is, 'making people happy', another three words.

Everything Disney do is designed around ***making people happy***.

- So when I'm working in one of their parks and I see someone's ice-cream fall off their cone, how and I going to make them happy?
- When I see a queue how am I going to make people happy?
- When there's a problem with a lost child , how am I going to make people happy?

It's completely empowering and invigorating.

For more information please look at *http://www.businessplans.org/mission.html.*

Now, this is becoming more and more important with the Internet empowering the customer and enabling them to see the reality behind your business. You are truly transparent – if you try and pretend that you're something you're not, when the customer sees through your veneer you're dead in the water.

It's important to treat this seriously and get it right.

So many businesses make the glib phrase, 'people are our greatest asset' or 'customers come first' ... without actually meaning it or doing anything realistically to make it happen.

Continual use of this type of phrase, and mission statements thought up by the board or marketing department on an awayday have almost become an automatic cue for cynicism rather than celebration from the customers, and very often you have to wonder whether those people making such statements are trying to convince themselves as much as anyone else!

This is why 'mission statements' have such a bad reputation.

Don't be like them – **believe that this has real value**, follow the rules below to discover and refine this and then use it to align strategy, systems, processes and behaviour ... obsessively.

The organisations that do mean it, prove it, not through glib phrases and 'marketing speak' but by making it simple and clear, using it incessantly and demonstrating it in every day behaviour. They will have a customer-focused mission that everyone knows and believes.

So it's true that people are your greatest asset but you have to prove it through what you do rather than just paint it on the side if your vehicles!

The first step to doing this properly is to discover, refine, publish to, and empower everyone in your organisation around, your customer-focused mission. This is your belief system at the core of your business. This is what will drive your actions in any situation, no matter what. This is what will empower your people to make the right decision in difficult circumstances. This is what will stop managers and leaders running away with their own ego. This is what will get things done. And this is what your customer will see again and again, and will keep coming back for more of.

It is your organisational compass for hacking through the jungle of everyday life!

It is your belief that you are in business to provide a service so good that people want to pay you for it rather than the other way around ... of course!

To quote Ray Kroc from McDonald's

'If you work just for money, you'll never make it, but if you love what you're doing and you always put the customer first, success will be yours.'

Action

You'll need to <u>discover</u> (not invent) your customer-focused mission.

It is there, if you think about it, but don't try and force it – take some time over this and work it through. It will need to have the following attributes:

1. Short and simple (and in plain language): so people can remember it.
2. Empowering: so it's a compass for your people to guide them through the trials of everyday life.
3. Positive: so it invigorates your people.
4. Timeless: this is not a goal this is a belief system.

And the great example of course is, 'every little helps'.

- How do you discover it?
- You ask yourself what your beliefs are,
- You ask your stakeholders what their beliefs are,
- You measure your customer experience,
- What you want to know is:
  - What is so important, that if we don't do it, nothing else much matters?
  - What would we want a customer to say about us behind our backs?
  - We want to be known as the organisation that ….
- You meet and consider all of the outcomes of these conversations, and it evolves and you agree it over time.

When you have discovered it you need to publish it on everything and you need to **use it as a compass for judgement on all strategy, systems, processes, and behaviour,** because just publishing it wont do the trick. You're back on your 'people are our greatest asset' problem.

You've got to use it as a compass:

- A compass for your strategy, your processes, your systems, your behaviour management, your meetings and your communication.

Whenever you have a decision to make, always ask: 'Is this aligned with our customer-focused mission?'

• Because, if not, why on earth are we doing it?

Top tips

Here are some 'Customer Focused Mission' 'top tips'!

• *When you have your customer focused mission, spend time agreeing clear values that arise out of it*
• *Meet regularly to specifically discuss your CFM and check that you're generally 'on course'*
• *Use it to generate feedback (more on this later)*
• *Ensure ALL your people know and understand it (and why it's there)*
• *Ensure all your policies, marketing & communication align with it*
• *Make sure EVERYONE's behaviour models it ... from the top down*
• *Have visual symbols, stories and traditions that stem from it*
• *Always ensure anyone you hire wants to be aligned with it*
• *And those who don't... need to go ...*

So that's enough on customer-focused mission, that's known as principle number one of Great or Poor. **Have a customer-focused mission.**

So lets move on now to principle number 2.

7

THE CUSTOMER'S REAL NEEDS

Principle two is called, 'find your customer's real needs'. This is all about emotions.

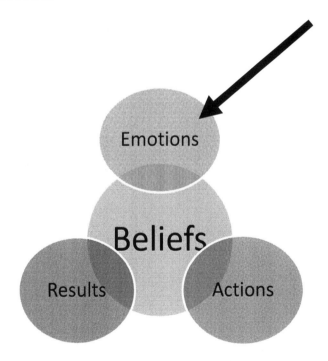

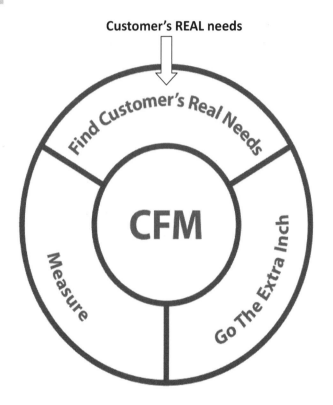

This is more like behavioural psychology rather than business training.

Because *customers are emotional and unpredictable* and all want different things, so it's a bit like throwing the dice when a customer comes through your door. You can get any result!

You've got to ask yourself, *'what do these customers really want?'*

And of course, these principles apply to ALL customers, both external and internal. How often do we think we know what our internal customers think or need, but when we spend a bit of time and attention on them we find out something we could never have known about or guessed?

Remember to treat your internal customers as well as or better than your external customers – if they don't feel valued or cared about, how on earth can they create this result with your external customers?

This principle works two ways:

- firstly: every customer is different, and will have different physical needs (so it's important to spend time and money on market research to understand customer trends and preferences)
- secondly: whilst their interaction with you will be based on physical needs, this will have an emotional need behind it – the key is to know what that emotional need is and to fulfil it what ever the situation

and the good news is: ***everyone has similar emotional needs!***

The Great or Poor system helps you with both of these:

- Firstly, by listening and caring about your customer (applying this principle excellently), you will naturally find out helpful information about your customer trends and preferences. But this needs a more systematic approach. In the fourth principle we will talk about measurements, and the system I outline there, if applied consistently, systematically and excellently, will help you gather clear, powerful, actionable customer feedback on their preferences, to help you continually grow and develop your business around customer's current and future needs.
- Secondly, by understanding this principle and ensuring all your people do the same, you will empower your people to communicate with your customers at their REAL emotional levels, and fulfil their REAL emotional needs ... and thereby build great customer experiences and outstanding customer loyalty

Now, remember the point we made in Chapter 2:

- **80% of customers will leave a product or service while being 'satisfied' with it**
- **63% of customers state that they left as a customer because of 'perceived indifference'**

This 2nd principle picks up these amazing statistics and turns them into an actionable plan.

You may well be familiar with Abraham Maslow's 'Hierarchy of needs'.

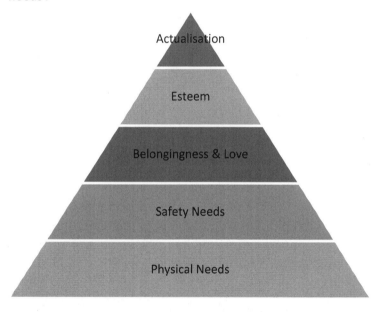

The basic idea is that people are physical beings driven by emotional needs, always trying to move up through the triangle. We'll be at different levels for different activities and at different times, but our drive is always to move upwards towards our needs of belongingness, esteem and actualisation.

This is good news for anyone trying to serve a customer (i.e. all of us), because all we have to do is know and understand this, and then learn what behaviours and skills we can use to help people move upwards ... no matter where we both start.

Of course, any business or team won't be in business for long if they consistently get physical or safety needs wrong, but for the purposes of this book, we're presuming that's not generally the case. There's not much point in aiming for consistently excellent customer experiences when you've not got the basics right!

Any organisation, team or indeed whole business sectors needs to get the physical and safety 'basics' right before trying to move upwards.

Now, you can apply the same principles to whole organisations, and create a simplified hierarchy of needs based on the market that the organisation is in, to help your people take the right actions to move your customers up the hierarchy, and thereby build great customer experiences and long-term customer loyalty.

Consider the following diagrams:

1. Remember the basic format of building a house?

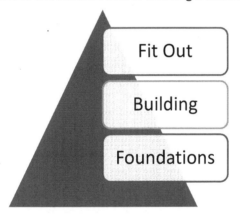

2. Now apply these same principles to a organisation:

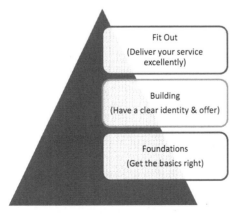

3. So this triangle perhaps looks a bit like this for any organisation – the customers of the organisation have a hierarchy of needs, based around moving up this triangle … and the starting point will depend on what the customer expects from past experience in this area of business (so, to use the old chestnut, we need to 'exceed customer expectations!').

Bingo!

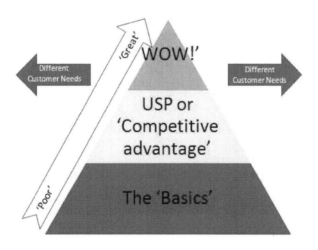

Here's a bit more explanation:

- At the bottom you have 'the basics': this is the starting point, if you don't get the basics right and you will be out of business very quickly. I don't intend to spend any more time on this for the purposes of this book – you will know what the basics are for your industry and if you don't get these right you won't be in business for long. I am sure there are plenty of instruction manuals in your business to tell you how to address the basics in an effective way.
- The next level is your 'unique selling point': another way

of describing this is your 'competitive advantage' – what's different about you? Why would people choose you over your competitors? What are you experts at? What can you do that no one else can? And, very importantly, what is it that you don't do and will never do? These are the fundamental business building blocks – you need to be sure of what these are and then move up to

- The top level: this is what we would call your 'wow' – what is it about the way that you do what you do that makes people talk about you behind your back is for the right reasons? This could be something major (for example, the 'wow' from Apple is the quality, innovation, and design), or it could be something minor (for example, the 'wow' for a small hotel could be to remember everyone's name and personal preferences).

The top level will build from the second level, which, in turn, cannot exist without the bottom level being right.

Interestingly, different business sectors have varying 'levels of success' in this diagram – in a highly competitive and transactional market (for example ebay, or supermarkets), you will generally have to perform consistently at the top of the pinnacle to stay in business, whereas in a less directly competitive market that may be more relationship based (and harder for the customer to switch suppliers), you may well be successful in the short term by just getting the basics right (for example some banks and professions may operate at this level, or any area where demand outstrips supply).

But beware, life gets more competitive every day, business becomes more transparent by the second, and supply is forever growing – you must keep moving upwards, wherever you start or whatever the 'status quo' in your profession. Otherwise, over time, you'll be dead in the water. For example, if we could put the clock back and do our shopping this week in the newest leading supermarket of 10 years ago, we'd be very unimpressed at the range, quality and service on offer ...

Back to the diagram. The top level is the key to your long term success and the pinnacle of the triangle. It's called being linked to your **customers' real needs**.

Now, there is one more slight complication to this diagram, based on the customer's real needs. The single most important thing from the point of view of the customer in their perception of what they would interpret as 'good service' is:

Consistency

- Without consistency, your business will be doomed to fail over the long term
- With consistency, you could deliver fairly mundane products and services, yet build a brand reputation that drives customer loyalty and ongoing profits – and, of course, the great examples of this are the franchised fast food operations around the world that we are so familiar with.

So the diagram really looks a bit like this:

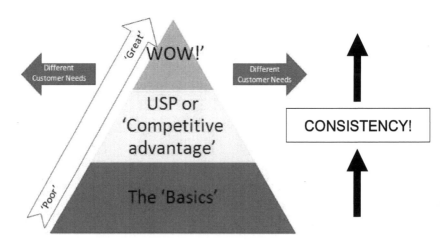

The first thing to remember about the customers' real needs is that customers value consistency above everything else – it is far better to be consistently mediocre than sometimes outstanding and sometimes appalling.

But of course, it's far better than that to be consistently great. With a global market, empowered customers, supply outstripping demand, and low cost competition springing up overnight, the levels between 'the basics' and 'USP' and 'wow' are for ever getting higher – what is great to day will be standard tomorrow, and if our organisation is not continually evolving and improving we will soon be out of business.

So what are the customers' real needs that will take them up this hierarchy towards a 'WoW!' experience?

These needs are probably not what you think they are.

We are always delivering an emotional need through a physical service.

So we need to stop and think deeply. What's the real emotional need for the customer in my business? What is a customer REALLY needing from my product or service? What feeling does my customer REALLY want from interacting with me? What's the critically important factor of my offer that needs to be delivered above all else?

Here are some examples for you.

- If a customer goes to a hotel their real need is not a bedroom for the night and a meal, they expect that as a matter of course. What their real need is to 'feel looked after' (research shows that it's often a need close to being cared for by a parent or the even more ancient need of being accepted by a new tribe!).
- If a customer goes to an accountant, their real need is not to have their books done or to get a set of figures, they expect that as a matter of course. What their real need is to 'feel peace of mind and to trust their accountant unequivocally'.
- If you are a customer of a stationery supplier your real need is not pens and pencils, you expect that as a matter of course. Your real need is to 'have your life made easier and to be able to trust this supplier (for example for price and value)'.

- If you are a customer of a takeaway pizza shop, your real need is not a pizza, you expect that as a matter of course. Your real need is that they will deliver the right goods, in the right time (which generally means speed is critically important in a business like this), i.e. 'they'll be quick (attentive) and they'll make your life easier'.

Moments of truth

Every time a customer interacts with you they have what is called a 'moment of truth'. This their **emotional experience** at this point. We are all the same – what we experience emotionally we will believe is 'true'.

Every customer will have a number of moments of truth in every transaction – the larger the transaction or relationship, the more moments of truth there will be.

The key challenge is to meet the customer's REAL needs at every moment of truth, and then to put systems, processes and training in place to ensure every moment of truth is addressed effectively going forward.

So the customer's real need is based on their emotions at their moments of truth ... so I can hear you asking: 'How do you know what these needs are and how do you address them ... there are so many moments of truth, and all our people are individuals ... this sounds like it can be bit of a nightmare?'

The answer is: don't panic – keep it simple and do it well...

In essence all customer needs can be boiled down to three things. (This is more good news, because, by focusing on these three things, you can keep it simple for your people, and empower them to deliver this result within your guidelines ... no matter what situation they're in!)

The first thing a customer wants is to trust you.

The great organisation that has made a phenomenal success out of strangers trusting each other is Ebay. They realised that when strangers trust each other business goes like a rocket.

So need number one of your customers is they want to trust you. If they trust you they will want to do business with you.

Trust is built out of two skills: character and competence. You have to have both in order to be trustworthy. The diagram below illustrates:

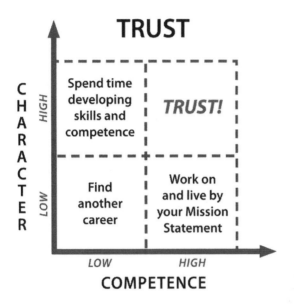

But they have other needs as well, a great customer experience has to be a bit more than just trust.

The second customer need is for you to make their life easier or better.

The organisation that did this brilliantly was Google.

Google won the battle of the search engines by making searches easier and better and Google spread virally around the internet because people said, 'you've got to try these people, they're great'.

The same has now happened for social media sites such as facebook and twitter. The key ingredient is that they make life easier or better and are easy to use.

The third need is for individual attention.

Customers want to be treated as an individual, not a number! It really is very simple. But, of course, the simpler it is to understand, very often the harder it is to do ...

This is obvious at the behavioural level, but it becomes much easier if the organisation's strategy is aligned around achieving this and all processes and systems are designed to help empower the individual to do this, and to achieve this systematically every day.

Here are some great examples of this in practice:

- Supermarket loyalty cards that personalise offers to you according to your buying habits
- Hotels that personalise your room according to previous occupancy habits
- Restaurants that remember your name and preferences
- Websites that make buying suggestions based on previous buying habits
- Call centres that make it easy to speak to a real person (and the right person) and have the right information on their screen
- Front line people empowered to solve problems on the spot, rather than having to refer to a manager
- Front line people who have been trained in empathic communication skills

So, you can see, this is a mixture of systems (of which CRM systems are the most helpful), processes and behaviour – but the important thing to remember is that the behaviour comes after the systems and processes. If you try to change the behaviour without aligning the systems and processes it can be somewhat stressful for all concerned. The best way to address this is to **go the extra inch** (more later).

In order to make this simple truth a reality in your organisation you need to have systems based on this, resources to do this, individuals trained on this, and feedback measuring this. This is what the Great or Poor system empowers you to do.

One organisation that has done this excellently is Amazon – through effective customer-focused systems, they build an individual relationship with you, manifested in actions such as recommendations of products when you buy something. Not bad for an organisation that's 100% online.

This, by the way, is the KEY area where small, individually run businesses can (and often do) outperform the big boys. If you're small, you can't compete on price, marketing and high powered selling systems, but you can compete on Individual Attention ... in fact it's probably what you'll have to do in order to survive.

(Note: these three needs are vital in every transaction, but vary in importance according to the type of business. For example, when a business is more 'transactional', this 3rd need is less powerful – customers will be happy if the first two REAL needs are met, but it's always there in the subconscious, and those who do this best will be the winners over the long term ... just as Amazon and Ebay have demonstrated).

So customers have three REAL needs:

1. **They want to be able to trust you.**
2. **They want you to make their life easier or better.**
3. **They want individual attention.**

If you do those three things then you will be at the pinnacle of the triangle and meeting the customer's real needs.

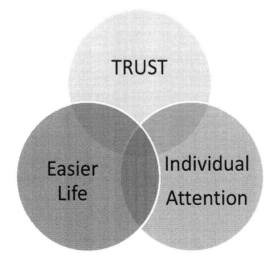

How do you find out how to do this? You have to gather feedback, listen and consider the answers empathically (more on this later).

Customers aren't interested in your needs, they're interested in their needs – the only way to get your needs met is by considering their needs first. Through doing this well, you will find the answer to meeting your needs. This is called 'effective communication' and of course blindingly obvious common sense!

This is not a book on communication skills, but here are the basics that you need to know in order to meet and exceed your customers' REAL needs.

Effective communication

There are various levels of communication, and what we're talking about here is developing skills to allow your people to communicate empathically – this means communicating in order to understand the other person from the other person's point of view (not yours) … so you can find out what their REAL needs are.

Like everything else to do with 'customer service' this is common sense, but how often is it common practice? We're often so busy considering our own needs that we haven't got the time or inclination to communicate empathically, listen and consider with no hidden agenda, and really get to the pinnacle of the customer's REAL needs.

There has, of course, been lots of research into what are the 'key things' the customer REALLY wants from your organisation, which contribute to their feeling of trust, attention and having their life made easier, but no two businesses have identical issues and no two customers have identical needs ... you need to develop your own systems and processes around what's right for your business by listening to your customers, measuring their experience, and gathering helpful feedback (all of which is covered later under principle 4 : **measure**).

Your people will also have strong opinions on this as well ... particularly those whose role is mostly customer facing! Just look at the amazing information bosses discover when they go 'back to the floor'. They should already know this! You need to be asking both your customers and your people their opinion on a regular basis – of course managers and leaders should always spend time 'back to the floor', but it should be done systematically, not once in a blue moon.

For example, the MD of very successful nationwide sandwich chain always used to work two shifts per week in his shops ... this is called 'Management by walking about' and 'leading by example'.

How to find out a customer's REAL needs

The best way to find out a customer's REAL needs is to look for body language and listen for voice tone and inflection that indicates that the customer isn't comfortable – these are indications for you on where your 'moments of truth' are not delivering the customer experience that is needed to drive loyalty and sales. Then you employ effective communication systems and skills to find out the REAL need without upsetting the customer or promising something you can't deliver.

If you don't directly interact with your customer, either in person or over the phone, you'll discover this through changes in buying patterns, timescales for purchases, return rates, and various other key information for your business. I'd also recommend you use the 'Great or poor score' (which is detailed later on) to help you gather helpful feedback and data on what's going right and what's not. These will also all be great indicators of where your 'moments of truth' are not delivering the customer experience you both want and need.

However you 'listen' to your customers; when there's a shift in behaviour or any of the other danger signs, don't ignore them – embrace them and get closer to the customer to find out their REAL needs and what you can do to meet and surpass them. Just by doing this, you'll be building customer loyalty!

This is not a book on body language, but this is well worth studying, for it forms the majority of REAL communication. Suffice it to say here that:

- People don't generally say exactly what they're thinking, unless they trust us completely
- So they often say one thing, but mean another
- It's our job, if we want to serve them well, by meeting their REAL needs, to find out what their REAL needs are, and then deal with them appropriately
- We sense these issues subconsciously through behaviour change, body language, tone and inflection in voice, and other emotional signals that we are all programmed to pick up
- All we need is the consideration to recognise them, courage to deal with them, and skills to deal with them effectively ... through communication

Perhaps it's easiest to think of this as 'peeling an onion' – the communication starts at the outside layer, but the real issue is hidden at the core. You have to have the communication skills to peel down and reveal the core so the real issues can be addressed.

This can be done by empathic listening combined with open questioning, all done in a spirit of compassion and integrity.

A good exercise to do with you people is to explain this 'peeling the onion' issue, and ask them for suggestions of what subconscious signals they can pick up from customers, how they can pick these up and start to address them and what they consider as good listening skills, and what questions work best for peeling back layers.

Communication processes

Here is a simple suggestion of a 'communication process' that will help you keep in touch with your customers REAL needs (both internal and external), that you can adapt to suit your particular organisation and situation:

Daily	• Key information briefings
	• Management by walking about
	• Catching people doing things well
	• Ad hoc coaching and holding people accountable
	• Listening to your customers through every channel you can: internal and external, structured and unstructured, direct and indirect, and having a coordinated systematic approach to this (see later when we discuss how to **measure** customer experience).
Weekly	• Go the extra inch sessions (see next chapter)
	• Sharing of key top line figures
	• Review of customer feedback from the 'great or poor score'
Monthly	• Focus sessions on 'Customers REAL needs' (see below)
	• Sharing of bottom line figures (including the 'great or poor score')
	• Monitoring progress on key goals
	• Coaching and accountability reviews 1:1 on key goals
Quarterly	• Personnel reviews using simple 'win/win agreements'
	• 'Blue sky' sessions on key process issues and opportunities
Annually	• Reviewing the CFM
	• Agreeing 360 degree targets for the following year

A list of ingredients

Here's an incomplete list of some of the main ingredients of 'trust', 'easy life' and 'individual attention'... (every organisation and situation is unique), with a simple exercise you can conduct with your people on a regular basis to keep clarifying and aligning processes with the customers' REAL needs systematically from now on!

Customer need (to have attention, build trust and make life easier)	MOMENTS OF TRUTH	
	What MUST we do (to get the basics right)?	What SHOULD we do (to be 'special')
Understanding: do we have systems and take the time to REALLY listen to and understand our customers?		
Enthusiasm: do we have systems and the right attitude throughout the organisation to ensure the customer is treated enthusiastically ... no matter what?		
Reliability: are we reliable in all that we do – do we have systems that drive actions, rather than leave it to 'common sense'? Do we have systems to ensure any issues are resolved reliably?		
Empowerment: are our people trained and empowered to deal with customers at the REAL level, or are they just 'doing a job'		
Follow up: do we have a systematic follow up process? Do we measure it? Do we do it no matter what?		
Visually attractive: are all our appearances visually attractive and joined up? Do they project an efficient and trustworthy image?		

Clarity and transparency: Are we clear on what we do and don't offer? And why? Are our charges clear and consistent?		
Extend trust: do we extend trust to our customers? Or do we treat the 99% like the 1% who will mess us around?		
Track Record: what's our track record? How will customers know? How can we show that we will deliver excellently without looking brash?		
Service Charters: internally and externally – do we have any? Are they customer-focused? Do they build trust, and make people's life easier?		–
Guarantee: what do we guarantee? How will we resolve issues? How can we give the customer confidence that they can do business with them for no risk?		
Complaints & Feedback: Do we welcome them or avoid them? Do we take time to deal with them effectively? Is everyone trained and motivated to do this? Is the customer rewarded for giving you feedback?		

Note: this exercise carries on in the next chapter, under 'go the extra inch', where we ask one more question: 'What COULD we do (to wow the customer)?'

How to make this principle work for you in your organisation

As ever, don't try and do this all at once – this is a marathon, not a sprint. Attention to the customers' REAL needs will help you identify these moments of truth, and going the extra inch (see next chapter) will empower you to address them.

Here is a simple process that might help:

1. Spend time training everyone (especially in your induction process) on this point – ask them for their views on what the customer REALLY wants. (Incidentally, this is a wicked question to ask candidates in an interview …)
2. Remember the old chestnut: any chain is only as strong as it's weakest link – start with your weakest links! (These will be identified from internal and external customer feedback and moments of truth).
3. Plan a timetable to review 1 system or process at a time on this point – weekly would be great, but monthly is probably more realistic in most circumstances.
4. Plan and agree 1 change at a time* – don't try and bite off more than you can chew.
   - Implement
   - Test
   - Finalise
   - Communicate
5. Then do the next step!

Note: people often ask me, 'How do we actually achieve this? We're so busy every day, that we never seem to have time to review our systems or processes, unless they're really causing a problem …'

My response is: when you know they're really causing a problem, it's already too late – they'll have driven off customers in droves. You need to get ahead of yourselves. Most organisations seem to have time for endless (and often pointless and largely unproductive) monthly meetings, so take the following actions:

1. *Organise these meetings better: using a meeting planner with the aim of reducing their time by at least 50%.*

2. *Then plan in one more short high impact meeting: MAXIMUM 1 hour.*
   a. *Call it your 'customers' REAL needs meeting'*
   b. *Identify one area of potential problem from your feedback and listening (a moment of truth)*
   c. *Get each attendee to do some specific research on this before the meeting*
   d. *Have a clear 'desired results' statement for the meeting (based on the customers' REAL needs from this moment of truth)*
   e. *Plan a simple and fun exercise to address the real issues and find some solutions*
   f. *Then implement and test (as mentioned above)*
3. *Some suggestions of exercises you can do*
   a. *Problem / consultant 'speed dating'*
   b. *Blue sky voting*
   c. *Choosing your 'word on the street' for this moment of truth*
   d. *The 3 levels of customer expectations: ideas for each one with this moment of truth*

   e. *The 5 whys*
   f. *Peeling the onion through questioning and listening*
   g. *Self motivated work teams with win/win agreements*

h. The customers' REAL needs triangle: key outcomes in each segment

i. There's LOTS of ideas on simple 'problem solving workshop techniques' available free on the internet. Have a look at www.businessballs.com for some inspiration, or email us info@greatorpoor.com and tell us what you want to achieve – we'll send you some simple ideas.

Conclusion

If you do all this well, you will get to a 'win/win' outcome with your customer, whereby they'll be pleased to trade with you, and you'll make a fair and growing ongoing profit from trading with them.

Without having persistent attention to the customers' REAL needs, the best you can hope for is good luck ... you might be lucky and be getting a win at the moment, but, over the long term, the ONLY sure route to success is by operating a win/win model based on your customer's REAL needs.

Action

So you need to ask:

- What are my customers' REAL needs in my organisation?
- How can I address these better than my competition?
- Where are my moments of truth?
- Am I continually looking for them and putting improved systems and processes in place to ensure the customers' real needs are continually addressed in them?

Continually consider:

- Are the processes that I've got here, is the strategy that I am employing, are the resources in place, are the systems, and is my people's behaviour enabling my customers to trust me and am I giving them individual attention and making their lives easier or better?

- Are we SYSTEMATICALLY working on our systems and processes to keep developing and growing? (Because, if not, we're becoming obsolete).

Because *if the answer to any of these is no, your customers will be looking for a different supplier.*

1. Start by having a meeting and asking all your people the first two questions from the 1st list.
2. At the same time, start surveying and listening to your customers using focus groups, meetings and the 'great or poor score' (more on this later).

Doing both these actions will start to address this.

Then what you do is: meet regularly to discuss the feedback and agree one change at a time, that you are all committed to, that will take you one step forward towards ensuring that every customer interaction with you is outstanding. The communication process set out above will guide you on how to do this, but if you do need any help and advice, please do contact us at *www.greatorpoor.com.*

This is similar to the Japanese principle of 'kaizen' – a process of continuous improvement that, over time, will result in excellence. This is called 'going the extra inch', and is of course common sense ... principle number 3 of great or poor.

Kai   Zen

Change   Good

The better you get at knowing your customer's real needs, the more useful this will become. As these needs materialise and clarify, and as people understand them, they can then become a filter for you, to help you make sound judgements in all that you do.

- A filter for your strategy
- A filter for your systems and processes
- A filter for your behaviour

If you filter all these with genuinely good intent, you will never go far wrong!

Filter everything through your CRN

Here are some 'Customer's REAL needs' 'top tips'!

- *Make sure you know what the physical needs were 3 years ago and how they've changed*
- *Take time regularly to consider what these needs will be in 3 to 5 years time*
- *Ask how you can make your offer relevant and interesting to these future customers, without alienating the existing ones*
- *Ensure people consider and know the difference between 'expressed' and 'unexpressed' needs*
- *Make sure people know your overall strategy and 'key business drivers' and how and why these relate to your customers' REAL needs*
- *Observe and learn from winners: inside and outside your organisation and business area*
- *Look for ways to customise and personalise what you do to 'wow' your different customer groups*
- *Track client data and behavioural changes to help you continually improve*

So that is principle number two, **know your customer's real needs**.

Lets move on to principle number three, which is quite a big subject because this is where most customer service material kicks in.

8

GO THE EXTRA INCH

This is the 'action point' of 'great or poor' – this is where the thinking and mindset shifts stops, and real action takes over.

We are moving from 'beliefs' and 'emotions' onto 'actions'.

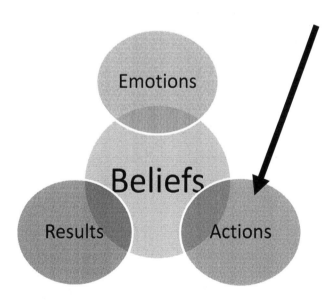

Go the Extra Inch

'As long as you keep on improving week by week, that is all that matters.'
(Lewis Moody, England International Rugby Player)

There's lots of valuable 'customer service' material out there, I am not putting any of it down, however it tends to all be ONLY about what do you ***do*** (or ***'actions'***). Do this, do that, smile at people, shake peoples hands, answer the phone within three rings, whatever it is. Well yes, we all know that stuff, it's what we call 'blindingly obvious common sense'.

Again the problem is, why doesn't it happen?

The answer to 'why it doesn't happen' lies in the first two principles:

We haven't got a **customer-focused mission** and we haven't filtered all of our strategy, process and systems through the **customer's real needs**.

We haven't got our beliefs aligned, and we aren't considering our customers' emotions – so we cannot get the right actions (or, if we do, it will be more through luck than design!)

Do those two things FIRST and THEN people will be empowered to **go the extra inch**.

If you don't do those two things you're back with the problem of taking the horse to water but not being able to make it drink ... and we see this happening every day.

This 3rd common sense principle is about the little inch over time which, if applied consistently and excellently, produces a huge amount of progress towards our goals. If it isn't done, on the other hand, businesses that are thriving today will fade and die as time marches on and their competitors get smarter, more efficient, and most importantly more customer-focused.

People can go an extra inch in every thing they do every day (they can't do the mile, remember).

I always love a definition of failure and success by a successful American businessman and philosopher, Jim Rohn – and he said this:

'The definition of failure is small lapses of judgement repeated over time'.

Then he defined 'success' as:

'Small disciplines of effectiveness repeated over time'.

It's **small things multiplied by time**. This is critical key to success in any organisation, any person, and any situation.

There was a great quote from Mother Theresa of Calcutta, when she was asked: 'How have you achieved all these great things in your life?'. Her reply was simple, honest and empowering for all of us: 'I haven't achieved any great things ... just small things with great love.'

This is the true principle behind 'Go the Extra Inch'. None of us can do 'great' things; everything we do is small – each day is made up by countless small actions, and these are the key to our success in life.

When we have problems with other people, it's always the small things that matter. For example:

- Saying 'please' and 'thank you'
- Smiling
- Remembering things
- Encouraging people
- Doing what you promised
- Making eye contact
- Small acts of kindness
- Small acts of attention

In fact, without the small things, any big things can even become destructive and counter productive.

So often, organisations announce 'restructuring', or 'reorganisation' in order to try and keep up with the competition and become more profitable. But they are missing the point – this just slams their organisation into reverse for a while, gets in the way of delivering results and upsets and annoys both their people and customers.

For evidence of this, just ask anyone working in a public organisation after a change of government!

Success isn't something that you strive for. You may have heard the phrase:

What I am suggesting is that the **_journey should be one of extra inches consistently and excellently_** every day, week, month and year.

Now this works at all different levels:

- It works at the personal level: how can each of us be empowered and enthusiastic?
- It works at the inter-personal level: how can we communicate excellently with and support each other?
- It works at a team level: how can we work together effectively?
- It works at a departmental level: how can we organise ourselves to achieve greatness?
- It works at the organisational level: what is it we need to do to be 'great' rather than 'poor'?
- It works with your strategy, systems, processes and your behaviour.

They all need to be focused around going an extra inch all the time, consistently and obsessively. If they are, then you will constantly improve and deliver better and better customer experiences; if they aren't, you won't.

It's as simple as that!

Action
For your strategy, ask yourself:

- Is this based around continuous ongoing improvement, that will empower my people to continually get better in small aligned steps, or is it based on a wish list delivered from the board?
- Is it simple, empowering, measured, and achievable, or is it somewhat optimistic?
- Do your people know it and understand it and know exactly what they need to do each and every day to take continuous steps towards it, or is it something that you keep for use at board meetings only and then manage your people with carrots and sticks?
- Do you link all initiatives to your strategy and explain to people how they fit, or do you just give people tasks in the dark?
- Do your people know the score and how they can personally contribute to improving it, or are they just expected to 'get on

with it' no matter what?

For your systems and processes, ask yourself:

- Are they based around empowering your people to bend the rules, within guidelines, in order to deliver outstanding customer experiences, or are they set in stone and can only be deviated from with permission?
- Do they arise out of your customer-focused mission, or are they 'the way it's always been done in this business' or even just about maximising profit today?
- Are they focused on your customer's real needs, or have they built up over time as a reaction to issues as they arise?
- Do they have built in to them the ability to be reviewed and continually improved, or is this just left to the whims of directors?
- Do they include the express purpose of looking for and listening to feedback from internal and external customers continually, or is feedback seen as a nuisance?

For behaviour, ask yourself:

- Do your people feel empowered to take the right decisions in order to deliver great customer experiences within guidelines, or are your people scared of deviating from your processes and systems?
- Do your people feel empowered to make mistakes and own up to them without fear of reprisal (obviously, within reason), or are your people constantly hiding things to avoid being told off?
- Do you meet regularly to discuss 'going the extra inch', or are your meetings just about dealing with issues and telling people what to do?
- Do you catch people doing something well at least three times as often as correcting them?
- Do people feel encouraged, empowered, and motivated, or do they feel repressed, frustrated and disengaged?
- Do you lead by example and when confronted by an issue, ask

'What one small thing could I do now to make this a little bit better?', and continue on asking and doing along these lines?

In general, *do your strategy, systems, processes and behaviour* allow consistent progress along extra inches to *develop trust with your customer, ensure you pay them attention and make their life easier or better*?

Because, if not, you're probably doing the wrong thing, and, if you're not struggling now, you probably will be in the future.

You need to be asking everyone:

* What small things do we need to do to develop trust with our customers?
* What small things do we need to do to make our customer's life easier?
* What small things can demonstrate attention to the customer?
* What help do we need to give each other to achieve this?
* What systems, processes and behaviour get in the way of this?
* What small thing can we do to start changing them?
* How can we keep evolving and developing to resolve all this?

The communications process outlined in the previous chapter will help you get to grips with this, and you may wish to revisit the exercise suggested there, with one more question: 'What COULD we do (to go the extra inch and be 'great' by wowing the customer)?'

	MOMENTS OF TRUTH		
Customer need (to build trust and make life easier)	What MUST we do (to get the basics right)?	What SHOULD we do (to be 'special')	What COULD we do (to go the extra inch)?
Understanding:			
Empowerment:			

Enthusiasm:			
Reliability:			
Follow up:			
Visually attractive:			
Clarity and transparency:			
Extend trust:			
Track Record:			
Service Charters:			
Guarantee:			
Complaints & Feedback:			

So whenever you meet and whenever you put systems and procedures in place, you've got to ask yourself: How can we go the extra inch?

How can we develop trust? How can we make our customers life easier? How can we ensure the customer feels valued?

The 'Go the Extra Inch' meeting

Here's a suggestion of something you can start doing immediately – it's called a **weekly 'go the extra inch meeting'** . It will develop a continuous rhythm of improvement, in a department, in a team or across a whole organisation.

(Note: if you can't do this every week, do it every 2 weeks, or every month at a minimum … it will still work well).

Every week, every team or group should meet to discuss the following: each person has two minutes to answer the following 4 questions and be held accountable for progress by their peers (rather than by their manager):

1. **What one thing did I do last week that moved us forward an inch?**
2. **What one thing happened this week that was really great, and I want to share with everyone so we can all enjoy it and learn from it?**
3. **What one thing this week was a total mess up, that I want to share with people so we learn from it and don't repeat it?**
4. **What one thing am I going to do this week to move us, as a team, forward one more inch this week, (and what help do I need from other people at this meeting in order to do this).**
   (That then ends up with the first agenda item of next weeks meeting, i.e. how did I do on it?)
   (Note: point 4 is the single most important point of the meeting … this is where progress in your organisation actually happens … but it's only an inch. Rome wasn't built in a day – don't try and solve issues all in one bite, just look to move forward one inch per week on one issue per person. This is 'kaizen' in action in your organisation … small steps, done continually will result in huge progress over time. Anything greater will not happen and you'll end up with frustration and stop having the meetings.)

It's critically important that you have these meetings, and that they are kept **short and very sharp** – otherwise, they'll become a mess and you'll stop having them. Everyone can see theoretically why this would be such a powerful meeting, but so often people start this process and then give up because the meetings take too long and become infuriating!

The way to get round this is for the manager to lead this meeting and allocate two minutes exactly per delegate to get through the four points – I suggest you buy a stopwatch and hold people accountable to the two minutes strictly! Yes, the first few meetings will be a mess … but people will soon get the idea, and then this will become the most powerful process in your organisation to drive forward the customer experience, and drive your performance towards 'great' and away from 'poor'.

So one thing you must do is start having these regular 'go the extra inch' meetings based around those four agenda items.

Here are some 'Go the Extra Inch' 'top tips'!

- *Make this a key value in your Organisation: 'If anyone sees an issue, they own it'*
- *Always set stretching goals for empowered people*
- *Share all your key figures: people without the right information cannot be empowered*
- *Entrust everyone with financial responsibility: let them make decisions on how they look after their customer*
- *Empower them to run as self managed teams and make their own decisions*
- *And have very clear boundaries!*
- *Trust your people and focus on ways you can 'remove barriers' for them*
- *Train and share issues between departments ... no silos*
- *Share mistakes openly so everyone learns from them*
- *Create simple 'quality improvement teams'*
- *Be prepared through training and sharing*
- *Listen and lead by example ... no exceptions!*

So there you have it, principle number three, **go the extra inch**. Start using that as a phrase within your business. Start making it happen, because people will be energized and empowered by an extra inch and they will start doing it, but remember these things only work if you truly believe them.

This will happen if you explain and train them, then you do it with integrity yourself and lead by example.

Which brings us onto our common sense last principle: principle number four, which is **'measure'**.

9

MEASURE

*'The wonderful thing about not having a measure is that
failure comes as a complete surprise!'*
Sir John Harvey-Jones

If you want results, you have to measure progress and keep improving!

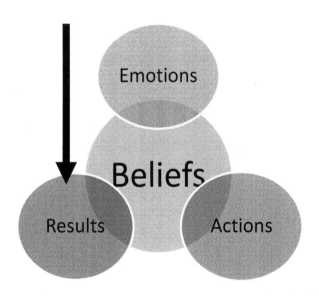

Because:

- *What gets measured gets done*, and
- If we can measure something, we can move it

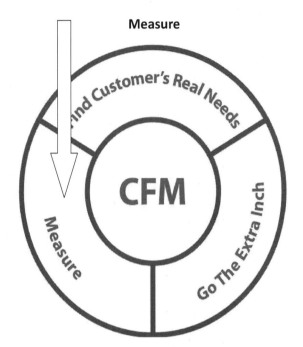

The first thing I do in seminars is to ask people this question:

What do we normally measure?

The answer to this, of course, is 'money!'

Now, don't get me wrong, it's very important to measure money … without it we can't survive. But it's an unbalanced measure – money is a measure of 'success today', we need a balancing measure of 'success tomorrow'

... otherwise we might be tempted to sacrifice success tomorrow in order to get success today (and does this ever happen? Of course it does! Every day!)

So we need to balance this with a measure of 'success tomorrow', which is, of course a measure of the 'customer experience'.

(Note: we may also have many other useful measures that relate to the 'customer experience' – for example, repeat customers, gratuities, or average order size, but we also need a specific measure of the 'customer experience' as it's own entity, to know how we're doing, motivate people, gain helpful intelligence, and stop us from shooting ourselves in the foot in the blind quest for success today!).

What we want is a measure that allows us to listen to the customers, find out their needs, get data to help us improve and measure progress along the way.

We want to:

- Listen to our customers because the main reason that customers leave is 'perceived indifference'.
- Find out their REAL needs so we can address this.
- Get data to help us improve, because if we stand still we will be overtaken by the competition.
- Measure progress because what gets measured gets done – our people need to know the score and find out what they need to do to move the score in the right direction.

Sometimes organisations try to achieve this through 'customer satisfaction surveys'.

So the next question I ask is:

'Why do customer satisfaction surveys not work?'

You can see that is a closed question which very few people challenge ... and I usually get great answers. Take a moment and write down your thoughts below:

```
.


```

Why don't they work? Well there's a huge list, and here are a few of the main reasons:

1. They're generally too long (they ask too many questions).
2. They're often marketing in disguise and the customer sees through them.
3. They ask questions from the company's point of view rather than simply asking the customer for their opinion.
4. They have no measurable output in the form of a score.
5. They are far too infrequent (and therefore somewhat pointless).
6. Because they are long and involved, it takes ages to get the information back to the people who need it – so they are often out of date before they are even published!
7. They don't produce simple actions that people can actually do – they generally produce a load of data that is just confusing! If you want people to be able to go the extra inch, they have to have information as to what that inch is!

What customer surveys often result in is low response rates and poor levels of feedback and completely dis-empowering and annoying results.

Most customer satisfaction surveys don't really work

In fact, it's even worse than this. Not only do most customer satisfaction surveys not really work, but also they often destroy customer value in their execution ... madness!

The other thing that is incredible is that they're always called 'customer satisfaction surveys' ... **we don't want 'satisfied' customers we** want 'delighted' customers!   80% of 'satisfied' customers will leave us!

So it has to be more than just a 'customer satisfaction survey'. We have to ask our customers more than 'are you satisfied?', we have to ask them, 'actually, from your experience, are we "great" or are we just "OK"?'

So what I'm suggesting is a simple, quick, empowering, and **cheap to run** survey called 'the Great or Poor score'.

Before I go into it I will just ask you to consider this:

Just imagine your financial director or your accountant coming to a board meeting in your organisation. Imagine if they treated the measurement of the financial results (success today) in your organisation in the same way that you maybe currently treat the measurement of the cause of those results (success tomorrow) – (i.e. poorly or not at all).

They might say something like this at a meeting: 'Well I haven't actually got any figures on our financial progress at the moment, but the bank manager hasn't phoned me in a few weeks, and I don't think we've bounced too many cheques, and I haven't had that many irate suppliers on the phone, so I guess things must be basically OK.'

I don't think they'd be very popular!

The incredible thing is that that is what many organisations do when they measure customer experience, if they even consider it.

So we've got to do better than that because that's kindergarten stuff.

What I'm saying is that 'customer experience' is the cause of the results and it's generally very poorly measured. Remember:

- Financial results are a great measure of 'success today'
- But *'customer experience' is the key measure of 'success tomorrow'*

The problem is that financial results are easy to find, concrete, very important to what's happening today, and easy to deal with – whereas 'customer experience' is hard to find, variable, hard to deal with, but critically important to what will happen tomorrow. The net result is that financial results always tend to override 'customer experience' results.

The finance director wins – we can so often sacrifice tomorrow to get the right figures today! This is commonly called 'drawn out suicide'.

We need a short but powerful measure.

It's got to be short because otherwise the customer won't want to do it, and it got to be powerful because it has to produce helpful and actionable results.

The measure I am suggesting is only three questions.

It is simple because it just asks the customer what they think. It's powerful because it delivers clear helpful actionable feedback, and enhances the customer's experience by asking them simple open questions and listening to their opinion without trying to influence it, rather than destroying it by abusing them and wasting their time.

Indeed, when we do these surveys for clients, we often find that their customers say to us, 'thanks so much for listening, it's great that someone's actually listening and caring'. This then often leads to an enhanced relationship between the customer and our client, resulting in more sales and more referrals.

Doing a customer survey well enhances the customer's experience and builds sales.

Doing it 'OK' or badly detracts from or destroys the experience and reduces sales ... It's critically important to do this well.

So, three questions, short, simple and powerful that builds and enhances your customer experience in the process. Who wouldn't want to do this?

Here are the questions:

Question one

Very, very simple. It's what we call the **customer-focused mission** question.

So, when we have our **customer-focused mission**, we ask our customer, *'did we do it?'*

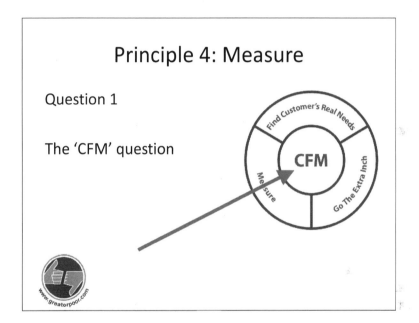

For example:

- if our customer-focused mission is 'every little helps', we might want to ask our customer: 'on a scale of 0 – 10 how helpful did you find us on this visit?'
- or, our customer-focused mission could be something like 'we aim to be the best supplier you deal with'. So the question would be: 'How do you rate us against your other suppliers?'

Very simple.

If we haven't got a clear customer-focused mission we can ask two things:

- We can either say, 'Based on your recent experience, how would you rate us, in general, out of ten?' (I'll explain how the scoring works in a minute).
- or, very simply, we could ask: 'Based on your recent experience, out of 10 how likely is it that you would trade with us / use us again?'

This first question is designed to give us a score of our 'customer experience'. So it's critically important to get it right.

How we get to a score is as follows:

Let's say we ask the customer to mark us 'out of 10'.

- 9 or 10 out of ten means we've done a great job, the customer will recommend us, they do think we're great and we're doing all the right things. We would call these people 'fans', 'partners' or 'advocates' – they are people who will build our business behind our backs for us for no charge ... fantastic!
- If we got 7 or 8 out of ten it means they are merely 'satisfied' – we've done an 'OK' job, but not a 'great' one ... these are the sort of people that are not going to leave you tomorrow, but **most of these people will disappear as customers over time**. These are a huge threat to your business and these people need to be looked after and moved from 7 or 8 out of ten to 9 or 10 out of ten. (How you find out what to do to achieve this will be explained later!)
- Then if anyone marks you as a 6 or below, these are the people who think you are 'poor'. Some of these people you'll never be able to help – you can't please all the people all the time, and it's good to know which ones you really can't deal with (so you can point them in someone else's direction, fulfilling their REAL needs, and thus avoid them wasting your time or ruining your business behind your back). But some of them you can learn from and either move them up in the scoring over time (by taking very quick remedial action) or learn from your mistakes and improve your subsequent service to avoid future damage.

The alternative way to measure this (and this is usually the best way to do it when you have a clear customer-focused mission), is to ask the customer to rate you as one of the following:

Definitely not	Probably not	Maybe	Probably	Definitely

The way to score this is simple:

- if the customer scores you as 'definitely', then this is the same as a 9 or 10 out of 10
- if the customer scores you as 'probably', then these are your 'satisfied' customers – the same as if they scored you as 7 or 8 out of 10
- if the customer scores you as 'maybe' or lower, these are your problems that you would deal with in the same way as the people who mark you as 6/10 or lower.

You can measure this in any way you choose, but I think the best, and most powerful way to measure this is to produce a score as follows:

1. take the percentage of people who mark you as 'great'
2. take away the percentage of people who mark you as 'poor'
3. you then have a percentage figure that will vary from -100% to +100% – this is motivational, because you can see movement quite quickly, and when you have a minus score it really motivates you to improve!

So we now have a score.

Note: this method of scoring is inspired by the 'Net Promoter Score' by Fred Reicheld (for more information, please see www.netpromoter. com). However, I do not recommend using the Net Promoter Score as a general tool, as I have found it to be rather general and inflexible. I also think it has limited use for public organisations and also for any organisation where they are consistently scoring 9 or 10 out of 10, as it doesn't dig deep enough to help these organisations continue to thrive and prosper.

Also please note that, in my experience, **it isn't that important** what method you use, as long as you do have a score and use a consistent and transparent method (based on your Customer-Focused Mission) to measure it. Whatever scale or method you do use, here are the key factors you need to consider in order to ensure it is effective:

1. The method should be consistent and clear
2. It must be aligned with and based on your 'Customer-Focused Mission'
3. Ideally, it should be able to be split down to relevant groups and individuals within the organisation
4. You should treat it with equal or more importance to your profit and loss figure
5. You must ensure it is demanding: don't kid yourselves that 'satisfied' customers are OK!
6. It should be displayed prominently, simply and clearly in your premises and on your website for all your internal and external customers to see
7. Your people should have goals and targets that align with it
8. They should be targeted to move it forward **(that's the crucial fact ... not where it is now, but the fact that it's moving forward constantly)**
9. This should be reviewed constantly and focused on incessantly at all levels
10. By hook or by crook, all your people should be motivated, incentivised and held accountable for ensuring that it does move forward

Question two

Question two is simple. What would you naturally want to ask a customer next? Of course, you'd want to ask them *'why?'*

So this is what you ask them.

You then need to ensure you get a REAL answer (ie they tell you about their emotional experience and their moments of truth).

- if you are doing this over the phone or even face-to-face, listen empathically to what they are saying to you, paying particular note to body language, tone, speed and inflection in their voice and take note of exactly the words that they use, being sure to question them when you are unclear (ONLY to clarify). It's critically important that you don't try to solve anything while getting the customer's feedback. The purpose of this question is just to listen and understand ... nothing else ... the customer just wants you to listen and care ... **please don't try and solve any problems at this stage!**
- If you are doing this electronically or on paper, please give them plenty of space to write down exactly what they want to say ... and it's always a good idea to offer anonymity (so they're honest), or the opportunity for you to contact them following the feedback, to sort things out / do more business / discuss other ideas / etc (ONLY if they want this).

The responses you get to this question will tell you what you need to know about your **customer's real needs**. This is the data that helps you understand your customer best. This is the information you share with everyone so that you know what your customer's real needs are, where your moments of truth are 'great' and where they're 'poor' and what you need to change in your strategy, systems, processes and behaviour in order to align with these needs.

Crucially, this also gives you that elusive positive feedback your people so desperately need, and rarely get enough of – so, really pay attention to this, and use this system to continually 'catch people doing something well'.

Question three
What else would you want to ask them?

Well, of course you'd want to know: *'what could we do to make your experience better next time?'*

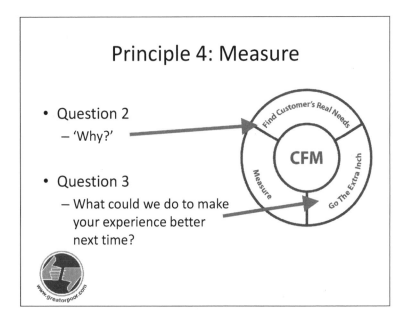

Not only does this help you build you business but it also implies that there will be a next time and that you want there to be a next time.

This is not manipulative ... as long as it is done with integrity.

This is where they will tell you how you can **go the extra inch** in the future (and, if there are major issues at the moment, this is where they will tell you what you need to do to solve them, and will usually give you the opportunity to do so).

Mainly, this question will give you valuable data on two things:

1. Ideas which you can use to look for **future customer needs and business opportunities.**
2. Specifically when you're generally 'great', this question gives you the data you need to continually keep improving – this is vitally important of course, as so many organisations rest on their laurels when things are going well, and only start to listen to feedback when things start to turn downwards ... which is usually too late ...

Question four

Unless there is a strong reason not to, you can now ask ONE more question: this is the question that we call **'The Ultimate Sales and Marketing Question'** and this is the whole purpose of the delivery of GREAT customer experiences.

'Customer Service' by itself is pointless (apart from making you feel good): let's get real: the REAL purpose of customer service is to build sales, reduce costs and create success.

When you have conducted your Measure with integrity (which is VERY important: without integrity, your customer will see right through you and the 'Ultimate Sales and Marketing Question' will not work ... in fact, it will work against you!), your customers will fall into 3 camps:

1. Those who thing you're 'Great'
2. Those who think you're 'Satisfactory'
3. Those who think you're 'Poor'

The 4th question you ask should depend on the answer to the first one.

- When the customer scores you as 'poor', the 4th question is: 'Would you like someone to contact you to sort this out'. As long as this is done with integrity, this will enable you to contact this customer following the feedback and turn a poor situation into a great one. Remember, *a problem well handled can turn the most critical of customers into loyal advocates –* this can be a great opportunity!
- When the customer scores you as 'satisfactory', the 4th question will be something like:
  - 'Can we call you again in X amount of time to see if we've improved' (Works well for a customer who has an ongoing relationship).
  - 'Can our market research people call you to find out more?' (This will help you improve and build customer loyalty).
  - 'Can we offer you X deal so you try our products and services again to see if we can do a bit better next time?' (Works well for a more 'transactional' type of situation)

- The 4th question, when the customer marks you as 'great' (or possibly at the top end of 'satisfactory' ... look and listen for body language to gauge what's appropriate) is a question that will:
  - build sales
  - build loyalty
  - generate recommendations & referrals

The question you ask will depend on your current business strategy. Be sure to ask them first if it's OK. Say something like:

'Is it OK if I ask you one more thing?'

If you have a specific new product or service, then by all means ask your customer their opinion of it (or whether they know about it) etc.

If you don't have anything specific you'd like to know, you can ask them ONE of:

- If they know of the other products or services you offer and if it'd be OK for someone to call them to talk about them
- If they'd like someone to call them to discuss any future needs
- If they'd like someone to visit them to find out what else you could do to help
- If they know of anyone else who might like to hear about your services ... and would it be OK to refer them for a testimonial if you contact them?
- If they'd 'recommend you' (and ensure you have a system to enable them to do this ... and if you want some help here, please do contact us), or give you a written (or video ...) 'testimonial', or
- Ask them if it's OK to put them on your 'special customer list' or suchlike. If you're looking to build sales through adding value and up selling to existing customers who think you're 'great' (a sensible strategy!) but don't have their email address already (eg in a shop, pub or restaurant). *[Note: PLEASE ensure anything you do send them is helpful and not a 'newsletter' or pointless information that only you're interested in. For more information, please look at www.greatorpoor.com for my article 'How to make social media actually work'.]*

Another option would be to ask them:

- Can you tell me why you chose us over anyone else? Or
- What was it about our offer that made you choose us?

Of course, both these questions assume you don't already know the answer to this question!

Alternatively, if you're doing this survey anonymously (which is a powerful way of doing it), or if you don't have data showing you the customer's current or potential turnover with you (for example in a hotel), a GREAT 4th question to ask is:

- How much do you spend on this (product / service) every year, and what % of that is with us?

I call this last ONE question (whichever question you ask) 'The Ultimate Sales Question', because this is what builds extra sales, cross sales, and referrals. It starts your remarketing to this customer.

But be sure to:

1. **Only ask ONE extra question.**
2. **NEVER start a selling conversation in the same phone call – this will then undermine the whole call. ALWAYS arrange to phone back at a convenient time.**

In fact I strongly recommend:

1. That the 'Great or Poor Score' call is done by a 3rd party for this reason alone (quite apart from the other benefits) ... (and we can offer this service).
2. That the 'Great or Poor Score' is done by phone by preference to any form of writing, as they key to whether it's appropriate to ask a 4th question lies in the response to the first 3 – so you need to be able to choose! (And very often, you'll only know through tone and inflection of the respondent, rather than the words they use.)

Remember, the purpose of the measure is to:

- Measure your service (the 'future profit' measure)
- Find out 'The word on the street' and what you need to do to keep improving it
- Motivate and empower your people
- Build long term customer loyalty

If you do this well, then you will have earned the right to ask ONE more question to help you build instant sales and extra marketing help.

PLEASE ENSURE: not only has this got to be done with integrity, but also you have GOT TO GET THIS 4th QUESTION RIGHT. This question will be different for every organisation, public or private, and every situation that the organisation is in. Please contact us to take advice on this. You only have 1 question to ensure you:

- Reduce customer churn
- Build marketing knowledge
- Increase sales per customer
- Build customer loyalty
- Increase referrals and recommendations

DON'T GET IT WRONG or, over time, they'll hang you ...

Other benefits of the 4th question:

This can give you really helpful data to prioritise your 'great or poor score' further. You can categorise all the feedback you receive like this:

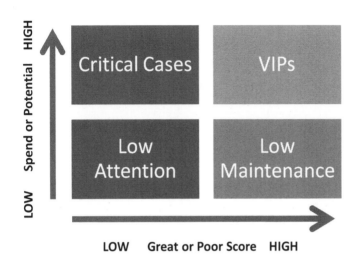

LOW   **Great or Poor Score**   HIGH

Of course, every situation is unique. It's worth getting professional advice and support so that you get this right … please see *www. greatorpoor.com* for further details and help.

Whatever happens, NEVER EVER ASK THEM ANY MORE questions! You know why this is … people have tried to ask you too many questions as a customer before … you know what it feels like!

This is not market research … this is a future profit measure!

Don't try and mix in some market research as well 'while you've got them'! You can ask them permission to do this later (which they are then much more likely to agree to)!

How to get high response rates:

So often I'm asked: how do you get such high response rates (with good data, we'd expect to get 85% + of respondents agreeing to participate)?

The key is as follows:

1. Remember your CFM: the purpose of this exercise is to genuinely listen to the customers, in the belief that if you do this well, and act on what you hear, you'll thrive and grow in the future ... NOT to conduct market research or sell them some more stuff!
2. Remember their REAL needs:
   a. TRUST: is this a genuine attempt to listen to them or is it PR or market research?
   b. EASIER LIFE: how long will it take?
   c. ATTENTION: will you just listen to them or will you jump in and try and sort stuff out?
3. Go the Extra Inch – start by:
   a. Telling them your name,
   b. Who you're phoning on behalf of,
   c. Why you're phoning (to 'find out what you think of us / them so that you / they can improve in the future'),
   d. How many questions it is (3),
   e. And how long it will take (Maximum 2 minutes),
   f. Then ask if it's OK.
4. Measure: response rates – and use experience to learn and improve

The value of this measure

The value of this sort of measure is:

a) you get very high response rates (it's quick and simple),
b) you get a score out of it (it measures your performance against your CFM) and
c) you can filter and assess the feedback that you get according to the categories of response, (and, if appropriate, categories of customer) to give you a list of clear actions to stop doing / start doing / and continue doing
d) you can track progress quickly and effectively over time
e) you can use the feedback to motivate and encourage people (they'll love it!)

f) you can hold people accountable to making these scores move forward

g) you can use this as a key performance measure (which I'd strongly recommend)

h) you get free business advice that you can act on!

i) It usually pays for itself many times over just as a by-product of doing it well and getting the 4th question right. (A good example of this was a customer of ours who invested circa £1000 a month with us doing exactly this, and saw immediate sales benefits of circa £13,000 per month every month on average! And this is just a by-product!!!)

And, above all else:

- By having a great, short and simple measure, that you execute professionally, all your people genuinely believe in and support, and that's customer-focused, meets their REAL needs and goes the extra inch, the customer (internal and external) will react very positively.
  - It builds loyalty because it shows you care
  - It gives them attention and stops them complaining to others behind your back
  - It genuinely helps you to continually improve (and that's VERY important ... no matter how good you are now!)
- And, most importantly:
  - The customer can accept that you make a cockup / are short staffed / have lost their order / have had a system failure / etc etc etc. This is called 'normal life'.
  - What they cannot accept is that you aren't listening and don't care.
  - *Having a great, short and simple measure and feedback system proves that you are listening and do care* (as long as you do actually use the feedback you get in a positive and effective way!)

Here's a quote from 'The Stupid Company'

How British Businesses throw away money by alienating customers (National Consumer Council Report 2008), by Philip Cullum.

The key message from our research is that companies need to do much more to understand what it feels like to be a customer. Indeed, customers themselves are usually only too happy to provide advice and information on how to get things right-so long as they are sure that someone is listening and is ready to act.

Sir Terry Leahy of Tesco says this approach has been key to his own success:

Our leadership team spends a lot of time in the front-line, not stuck in a chateau a long way from the trenches. I visit hundreds of stores a year, and I would say 40% of my time is spent in stores. I talk to staff a lot and I talk to customers a lot. I attend customer panels as a way of life.

We've developed many ways of giving customers a voice in the business, from Clubcard database management to market research, focus groups, panels, surveys – and so it is with staff. I used to work in marketing – and developed a number of these tools – but for me the most powerful thing is still listening to customers. The life they lead, the problems they have, and their experience in your stores.

All this information could just gather dust. But it doesn't, it's hard wired into the key decision-making committees of the company. The customer gives the leadership of the business the plain and simple truth about the business – it's the most honest feedback you ever get. In my experience, if you listen really closely they not only tell you what's wrong – they actually tell you what you need to do (and it's all free advice). Then what you have to do is believe them – and act on it!

'I want to labour this point. It isn't enough to use the language of the customer. You really have to believe the customer. This is where I think many organisations fall down. Because they only pay lip-service to the consumer, they never really find out where

their business is. They never learn where they need to be, and even when they do, they don't always have the courage to go there.

So there you have it:

People who mark you as 'great' will tell you about things that are important to them that you need to ensure are systematised and promoted. They will also give you plenty of ammunition to 'catch your people doing something well'.

The people who mark you as 'satisfactory' will tell you what you need to do, over the medium term, to keep going the extra inch and keep moving your business forward. This will be key information for your weekly meetings to help you continually evolve and improve.

The people who mark you as 'poor' will tell you two things:

- what sort of people your product or service is really just not suited to and
- where you are making some dreadful mistakes that you need to rectify immediately.

This measure is your powerful measure of 'future success'.

It empowers individuals and enables you to measure the performance of individuals and departments. It enables you to catch people doing something well and gives you a phenomenally powerful subject for your regular 'Go the Extra Inch' meetings.

It gives you all the data you need to:

- check progress on (and refine) your **customer-focused mission**
- understand and take action to align your strategy, systems, and processes around your **customer's real needs**
- know what you need to do to continually **go the extra inch**

But it only does this if you do it with integrity to the purpose ... and the purpose is to simply listen and understand their needs, not to leap in and solve them.

Sometimes, I have to say, it is really helpful to get a third party to do this for you, (and indeed we can provide this service). It is helpful to get a third party to do this because a third party will just listen, get the right information, ask open questions and build the relationship by just doing that ... not by trying to leap in and solve everything!

Using a 3rd party also has the following benefits:

1. **Honesty of data.** The customer just wants to tell you what they think, honestly ... without embarrassment or upset. The ONLY way you can be sure of this is via an anonymous survey conducted by a 3rd party.

2. **Provides perspective.** The 3rd party will see the feedback just as it is, and will be able to see the issues clearly and from an unbiased but expert perspective. No matter how objective you think you are, you'll filter feedback through your own emotions and desires.

3. **Cost-effective use of time and resources.** Your expertise lies in providing your service. Using a 3rd party to collate and provide customer feedback is both cost-effective in time, and avoids distraction and bias. Your energies are best used dealing with the feedback to improve your business, not in gathering it.

4. **Ensures integrity to the customer's needs and desires.** Again, no matter how 'objective' you are, you won't be able to resist the odd extra question here and there. This will destroy the exercise in the customer's view. The customer just wants you to listen to them ... nothing else!

5. **High response rates.** If you're paying for the service, you'll want to use it as much as possible. If you do it yourself it'll just be a chore and your mindset will be the opposite.

6. **A regular report with a 'score'.** Only a 3rd party can give you an objective score for you to use to motivate and encourage your people. Only a 3rd party will always produce a full report ... if you do it, you may be tempted to cut corners in these vital areas.

7. **Peace of mind.** Using a 3rd party ensures it gets done on time every time, and takes away another worry from you.

8. **Resource.** Using a customer service specialist means that you'll benefit from their input and resources to improve your business.

9. **Shows you're serious**. Using a 3rd party shows that you really do want to know what your customer thinks, and that you're prepared to invest money and time with a professional to do this. This builds loyalty in itself.

Remember: **we don't want 'satisfied' customers, we want 'delighted' ones.** Enough said…

Some tips to make sure the scoring is powerful and effective:

- Do it frequently: feedback from recent customers is more helpful than feedback from customers who haven't done business with you in a while
- Ensure that you prioritise feedback from large, frequent, or potentially large or frequent customers: it's more valuable!
- Make a simple and clear scoreboard and put it in a prominent place in your organisation
- Have the regular 'Go the Extra Inch' meetings to keep moving forward

These tips are important to consider when you get this scoring going. Don't worry too much about this at the start – the most important thing is to just get started!

Action

Of course, the action from common sense principle number four, **Measure**, is to *start measuring.*

Just by starting to measure, you will achieve an uplift in service and customer experience (remember, customers always want you to listen to them!), this is because this simple actions sends a hugely powerful and simple message to your people (and your external customers) … 'we're serious about this'.

But listening is not enough – you have to take action on this.

So the process is this:

a) Explain to all your stakeholders that you will be starting a measure and , most importantly, why you are doing it
b) **Train them in the Great or Poor system and thinking**

c) Tell them that you don't need anything from them at this stage, apart from to be aware of this, and to think about how their actions will impact on this

d) Start the measure

e) Start feeding back the results of the measure at meetings you already have

f) Over time: gain buy in and support from your people (you do this by using the information to catch your people doing something well, and by providing them with helpful information to improve sales that you glean from the customer feedback)

g) Make a large and prominent scoreboard (a good place to put this would be in your reception area and in your staff recreation area): be sure to change the score frequently (at the very least monthly). You can put other scores on this board (for example turnover or response times ... one or two key critical measures of your business), but don't make it busy – make it simple clear and empowering.

h) Consider introducing simple and fun incentives around increasing the score (but remember, what is motivational to one person may be demotivational to another ... ask and get lots of feedback from your people before you introduce anything).

i) Start the go the extra inch meetings and start taking action from the results of those meetings.

j) Develop your communications so you have a process that drives greatness (as suggested in Chapter 7

k) Then you'll have a SYSTEM to drive excellence and continuous improvement

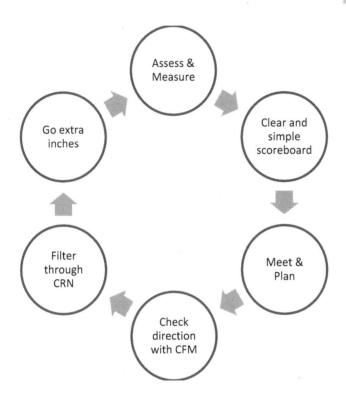

Final note: Social media and the power of the customer on the internet

As a final note to this chapter, it's very important to mention Social Media and the power of the customer on the Internet. Your customer is now empowered like nothing before via the power of feedback and gossip on the Internet – in the 21st Century, the experience you deliver to the customer is truly transparent.

By implementing the Great or Poor system, not only will you drastically reduce the chances of customers negatively affecting your business through gossip and poor feedback, but also you'll significantly increase the likelihood that the customer will tell YOU about any issues (rather than tweeting or facebooking it to the world instead).

By implementing these ideas, you'll be working alongside the customers' REAL needs, so they'll be much more likely to want to work with you and help you continually develop and improve.

Remember: the customer can understand that you can make a mistake and get it wrong, what they cannot, should not, and will not understand is that you don't appear to want to listen or care. The best way to listen and care is to have a simple and easy to use SYSTEM to help them feed back to you, and then use this feedback to improve.

Whilst all this is true (you know it is, because it's all common sense), there are two strong recommendations I'd make to ensure that you get it right:

1. REALLY commit to this as a new and better way of doing business. Invest some time and money in doing this – it'll be much more beneficial than yet another advertising campaign! Doing this well isn't expensive to do, but can be catastrophic not to do!

2. Alongside this, put systems in place to listen to customer gossip on the web. Then put all the data together to get a real picture of the 'word on the street' about your organisation. This is of course a specialist area, and is changing all the time, so, if you're unsure of what to do to achieve this, it's again worth employing a trusted 3rd party to help you.

The customer is king in the 21st century. Those that thrive and survive are not the strongest but those most adaptable to change – the best way to be ahead of the game on change is by listening very closely to 'the word on the street'.

The answer to success is very much in your hands ...

To access more information and services to help you survey customers effectively, please go to *www.greatorpoorscore.com*.

Here are some 'Measure' 'top tips'!

- *Put systems in place to listen to gossip on the web and especially social media.*
- *Join in with social media: don't let it happen without you!*
- *Make sure that customers find you easy to pass feedback to ... and welcome it!*
- *Consider all channels to make this happen.*
- *Consider simple, powerful, fun incentives around your measures*
- *Measure and listen to those who haven't used your services, or have stopped using them*
- *Regularly measure your internals customers' 'great or poor score' of their experience of your organisation*
- *Consider doing the same for all your stakeholders*
- *Develop 'collaboration metrics' that measure service between departments to each other*
- *Use all your data to improve processes, track buying habits, and personalise service*
- *Remember: measuring and listening is only valuable if you act on your findings!*

So my advice to you is this:

If you only do one thing from reading this book, start listening and measuring feedback from your customers.

If you do two things from this, start listening and measuring feedback from your customers and start having your regular 'Go the Extra Inch' meetings.

So there you have it, principle number four, listen and measure, and take action on that measure.

10

THE GREAT OR POOR SYSTEM: SUMMARY

Common Sense Principle 1: The Customer-Focused Mission

Overview of Common Sense Principle

- You will achieve what you focus on.
- Your people can only be empowered if they know what's REALLY important and are all aligned around one direction.

- Business (and life) is much more like 'hacking through a jungle' than 'following a map', so you need a clear, simple, empowering compass to keep you on course.
- By focusing on your 'customer experience' you deliver value for the long-term.

More Detail to Clarify

Focus on the customers and the results will follow, not the other way round.

The first step in customer service excellence is developing and ruthlessly sticking to a 'Customer-Focused Mission'.

In order to develop a 'Customer-Focused Mission' ('CFM') you need to ensure all stakeholders, and all policies, procedures and behaviour, without exception, are aligned around the 'Customer-focused Vision'.

And the 'Customer-focused Vision' should be something like:

'The only way we'll succeed is if we delight the customer consistently and excellently. The only way we'll do this is by having the guts and passion to do what's best for the customer at all times ...even if it may conflict with short term goals.'

Then ask, listen, share and refine – over time you'll discover your customer-focused mission.

As usual, it's blindingly obvious common sense and simple to understand, but it's often hard to do. This is because:

1. Managers and leaders have grand ideas, and often think it's their job to 'tell everyone' what the 'Mission' is. It isn't, it's EVERYONE's responsibility to obsessively ask their customers, and each other, what they think this is, and thereby 'discover' it.
2. Most 'Missions' mean nothing, they're just grand platitudes. So 'Missions' have a bad name for a good reason. But our research shows that you have to get this first step right in order to get everything else right.

Mission is about what we do and how we do it. It's all about:

- What we're going to do in order to deliver the 'Vision'
- What ideally we would like our customer to say about us to their friends and colleagues behind our back

.... and is often accompanied by 'values', which mean

- How we're going to do it

When an organisation has these clearly thought through and clearly communicates them, incessantly, to all stakeholders, they will then have 'alignment', and the foundations of success will be in place.

But beware: this takes time, commitment, effort, objectivity, passion and obsession. It cannot be 'done overnight', and just communicated to the people...

No involvement = no commitment

You will know when this really is working when everyone from the MD to the cleaner (both roles being equally important), can clearly state the Mission when asked, and can understand and find guidance in it for their role.

The story goes of the person sweeping out the hangar at NASA who, when asked what his role was, replied: 'I am helping to put a man on the moon'. Bingo!

A great Mission statement must be:

- Clear, short and simple (easy to understand for all stakeholders)
- Empowering (empowers all stakeholders to make decisions based on the 'Mission')
- Measurable (the measurement as shown in this book)
- Worthwhile (otherwise it will destroy the organisation)
- Directly linked to the 'Vision' (obviously)
- Customer-focused ... say no more!

And very often, a great Mission statement should be Timeless; it should be able to stand the test of time, and will usually achieve this by being based on timeless principles.

It's essential to get all this right. This is the root of everything your organisation does – the only way to get bountiful fruit is to have sound roots!

Example to illustrate

A restaurant in the UK has a customer-focused mission that says: 'Every customer should leave with a smile on their face, keen to return.'

This restaurant has increased turnover by 800% since they discussed, agreed and clarified their customer-focused mission.

- Everyone has this written into their contract of employment
- Every policy and procedure is written to achieve this
- Every member of staff is empowered to achieve this result, no matter what it takes
- This is measured consistently by using the 'great or poor score'
- Every meeting starts with this as the main aim

What you can do to 'make it a real'

This is what you do to discover your customer-focused mission

- You ask yourself what your beliefs are,
- You ask your stakeholders what their beliefs are,
- You measure your customer service, using the 'great or poor score'
- You meet and consider all of the outcomes of these conversations, and it evolves and you agree it over time.
- You review it regularly ... preferably annually

When you have discovered it you need to publish it, on everything and you need to use it as the compass for judgement on all strategy, systems, processes, and behaviour. It is your 'organisational compass'.

Stay true to your compass and you'll never get lost … take shortcuts and you can end in the swamp!

Common Sense Principle 2: The Customer's REAL Needs

Overview of Common Sense Principle

- Customers are emotional and unpredictable
- Customers have different physical needs, but similar emotional ones
- Customers want you to care about them and pay attention to them
- Customers will remember how they felt emotionally about your product or services, long after they have forgotten what those products or services were – these are called 'moments of truth'.

- If you connect with a customer emotionally, they will be loyal to you and will promote your products and services to their friends and colleagues
- If you abuse their emotions, they will do all in their power to harm you
- Customers have three overriding emotional needs from any transaction
  a) to trust you
  b) to have their life made easier or better
  c) to get individual attention

And one more thing ... customers are NOT always right; they are often wrong or difficult ... but they ARE always the customer!

More Detail to Clarify

We think we know what the customer wants (because we're the experts in our business) ...but we don't!

What emotions will your customers display if you get it very right?

Customers often make logical decisions based on emotional stimuli. In a word, they're 'unpredictable'! So it's very hard to anticipate their needs – yes, but we can predict their emotions.

For example, if I go out to eat in a restaurant, I don't want a meal, as I can get that far quicker and cheaper in a supermarket. I want: relaxation, or to be looked after, or some time out, a quiet meeting, or romance, etc., etc. So in order to deliver excellent service to me – and therefore fulfil it's CFM – the restaurant needs to work out what emotions I'll have if the above things happen.

...Probably 'happy and relaxed'!

So they need to align ALL strategy, processes, and systems around making the experience 'happy and relaxed' for the customer. Yes, the quality of the food, service and environment are important in themselves, but ONLY in as far as they produce 'happy and relaxed' feelings in the customer.

What, specifically, is important?

So often organisations spend a huge amount of time, effort and money in things that have no bearing on the customer's emotions (perhaps like advertising), and precious little on the things that do (perhaps like answering the phone quickly and efficiently, or essentially training and incentivising their people to 'make people's day'). This is because they haven't thought this through, aligned processes around delivering emotional needs above all else and haven't got a system to keep listening to the customers (at the deeper level).

So, all you need to do, in order to delight your customers excellently and consistently, is to think through what emotions your customer will display if you get it very right (i.e. deliver your CFM), then align all strategy, processes and behaviour around generating this ... and then keep listening, evolving and improving.

Not always as easy as it sounds...

Example to illustrate

A doctor's surgery had a problem with long wait times for patients.

Despite the best planning, very careful attention to ensuring that appointments were made at suitable intervals, and all patients being screened at the time of booking, appointments always overran, patients had to wait, and high levels of frustration were experienced.

After careful consideration and consultation, this problem was addressed by focusing on the customers' REAL needs. They actually understood that other appointments could overrun, and they might have to wait – they REALLY wanted to feel valued and cared for when this happened!

A simple, no-cost solution to a large problem that could have had a lot of money thrown at it to try and 'solve' it! And of course: common sense!

So,

- patients were warned in advance that waits could happen
- when a doctor was running late, the patient was apologised to, given a clear timescale, offered a refreshment, and even offered an appointment with a different doctor (if available)
- when this patient saw the doctor, the doctor started off by apologising for the delay, and assuring them that this would not affect the amount of time they had with them
- on leaving the surgery, the patient was again apologised to,

and asked if everything had been addressed as required (using the great or poor score)

By taking these simple steps, customer experience improved dramatically, and patients left much happier. It also had the knock-on effect of reducing delays, as patients began to understand the effect they had on other patients if they took too much time from the doctors! Truly, a win-win all round, simply by focusing on the common sense principle of the customer's REAL needs.

What you can do to 'make it real'

You need to ask:

- What are my customers' REAL needs in my organisation?
- How can I address these better than my competition?
- Where are my moments of truth?
- Am I continually looking for them and putting improved systems and processes in place to ensure the customers' real needs are continually addressed by them?

Continually consider:

- Are the processes that I've got here, is the strategy that I am employing, are the resources in place, are the systems, and is my people's behaviour enabling my customers to trust me and am I giving them individual attention and making their lives easier or better?

Because if the answer to any of these is no, your customers will be looking for a different supplier.

Start by having a meeting and asking all your people these questions. Then develop your communications processes as suggested, to produce ongoing consideration of this critically important question in all that you do.

On an ongoing basis, whenever you have a problem to solve, think deeply, don't just rush in to try and 'solve' it. Think:

- Who is the customer (or customers) in this situation?
- What are their REAL needs?

- What result are we all looking for?
- What information do we know?
- What information do we need to find?
- Who do we need to ask?
- How will we ask them?
- How will we put aside our own needs so we can best understand the customer's?
- What resources have we got?
- What other resources do we need?
- Who else could help?
- How will we measure progress?
- When will we review?
- How will we know if this has been successful or not?
- What will we do if it is successful?
- What will we do if not?

This is the principle of 'thinking deeply' about issues and processes, and aligning all solutions around your customer's REAL needs.

At the same time, start surveying your customers using the 'great or poor score ', as this will provide you with all that information that you aren't currently aware of.

Common Sense Principle 3: Go the Extra Inch

Overview of Common Sense Principle

- You can take a horse to water but you can't make it drink
- Small steps can be implemented excellently, but great changes often fail
- Small steps repeated consistently over time produce great progress
- Excellent customer experiences can only be delivered through systems and processes that continually evolve and improve to meet the changing and increasing demands of the customer

More Detail to Clarify

Customer service material so often mentions going the 'extra mile', but our research indicates that your people probably see this glib and meaningless phrase as demotivational. This is because it makes it seem hard and onerous, and it shouldn't be – it should be easy and fun.

...Because, if it isn't, it won't happen.

The other reason for the 'extra inch' is that the customer will be wowed by the little extras delivered excellently, consistently and positively, rather than the great things (that are so much harder to get excellent and consistent).

- A cup of tea, or a friendly piece of advice, delivered excellently, at the right time, when unexpected, will build customer loyalty better than any marketing budget could possible hope to achieve.

You can take a horse to water, but you can't make it drink. So it is with your people; you can tell them to 'go the extra inch', but you can't make them. In fact, the more you tell them, the less likely it is that they'll want to do it!

The only way you can get them to 'go the extra inch', excellently, consistently and positively, is by:

- Developing your 'customer-focused mission'

- Aligning everything around it
- Empowering and encouraging around the customers' REAL needs
- Measuring and feeding back
- And of course: Leading by example

As Jim Rohn famously stated:

> *'Failure is simply a few small errors in judgment, repeated over time. Success is simply a few small disciplines of effectiveness, repeated over time.'*

Help is At Hand

Don't worry, Rome wasn't built in a day – and neither was it built by one person. The key to the 'extra inch' common sense principle is that:

- everyone can do this at all levels
- this can be built into all the systems and processes
- people only need to change one thing at a time
- if you do this consistently and excellently around your regular 'Go the Extra Inch' meetings , you will achieve great progress over time

Example to illustrate

When the British rowing team for the 2000 Olympics in Sydney were planning on their strategy to win the gold medal, they worked out, on current form, what the winning time for their race at those Olympics would be.

They then worked out how much faster they would have to row, from current form, in order to win the gold.

They then split this improvement down into weekly targets, and worked at achieving these targets week on week.

By doing this, they manage to win gold.

This is a process understood and employed by top sportsmen around the world. It is also a process that is understood and employed by top performing businesses.

Take a leaf from their book: learn from them – the extra inch, consistently and excellently applied, is all that's needed. Continuous small improvements, over time, produce fantastic results.

What you can do to 'make it real'

When you have your meetings, and are trying to resolve issues, following on from the actions suggested in principle two, you need to be asking everyone:

- What simple small step could we do now in order to develop trust with our customer?
- What simple small step could we do now to make our customer's life easier?
- What help do we need to give each other to achieve this?
- What systems, processes and behaviour get in the way of this?
- What small step can we take to start addressing this?
- How can we keep evolving and developing to resolve all this?

And, of course, you need to be having regular 'Go the Extra Inch' meetings to empower everyone and continually drive improvement towards consistently excellent customer experiences, week on week, ad infinitum!

For more advice and free information on this point, please go to *www.gotheextrainch.org.*

Common Sense Principle 4: Measure (and act on the results)

Overview of Common Sense Principle

- What gets measured gets done
- If we can measure something we can improve it (if we can't, we probably won't)
- Money is the result of other actions: in order to get more money we have to measure the actions that cause the customers to want to give it to us!
- Feedback builds customer loyalty and reduces the customer's need to tell everyone else when you get it wrong!

More Detail to Clarify

Many customer service measurements are lame and pointless at best, and very often have the opposite effect to that intended.

This is because:

- They ask too many questions
- They ask the wrong questions
- They annoy your customers (rather than build trust with them)
- They have low response rates
- They are hijacked by the marketing department
- They have no meaningful score
- They are not regular, so no one can see what progress is being made
- They provide little helpful feedback
- They look for 'satisfaction' (and we don't want this!)

The key is to ask the customer:

1. *Have we achieved our CFM?*
2. *Why?*
3. *What else could we do to improve your experience?*

If we ask these questions, we'll have the score, along with the qualitative feedback we need to develop our organisation towards excellence.

When we've asked these 3 questions, and got 'great' feedback, we can then ask 'The Ultimate Sales Question' to continue the relationship and build our business through repeat sales, selling up, cross selling and referrals. This question will depend on your strategy, but will be something like:

- Can we call you to discuss other services we offer?

And remember, doing this type of surveying is an area where the input of a third party is essential – it will give you high quality honest information, a meaningful score, perspective on your business, high response rates, regularity, and, above all peace of mind. Using a 3rd party is also a huge message to all within the organisation that you're serious about getting this right ...and it can be done very cost-effectively.

This is too important not to do, and not to do well.

Example to illustrate

A wholesaling company started using the greatorpoor system, including the score.

When they started, sales were declining at around 17% per annum.

They started by discussing, refining and agreeing their customer-focused mission – this was done successfully, and added great value. They then started to measure.

Using the measure, they discovered some key things that they were doing that was causing their sales decline, and some key things that their competitors were doing that they didn't know about.

So they changed a number of systems, processes and behaviour in order to address the gap ... and have kept changing, evolving and improving ever since (by using the 'great or poor score')

Within 12 months, the sales had improved, and were looking healthy. So much so that this company then took over another company.

After takeover, service levels decreased significantly for a short time. This showed up immediately in the great or poor score, and management were able to take quick action to minimise the damage. This was done effectively and sales improved again.

The key benefits were:

- the board knew what sales would do in the future, and could plan accordingly
- service issues were picked up very quickly and addressed via weekly 'go the extra inch meetings'
- a great focus was placed on 'catching people doing things well'
- morale and empowerment grew significantly as a result of the above three points
- sales decline was turned into sales growth in under a year
- on top of this, previously lapsed customers were reinvigorated into becoming current customers, simply by being asked for feedback (this in fact has become a huge sales builder for this Company and others – just by asking the customer, they build the relationship, and gained significant incremental sales!) This alone justifies the cost of this exercise ... and it's just a by product...
- they continue to use the score to boost sales, morale, and profits successfully

What you can do to 'make it real'

The process is this:

a) Explain to all your stakeholders that you will be starting a measure and , most importantly, why you are doing it

b) Train them in the Great or Poor system and the thinking behind it

c) Tell them that you don't need anything from them at this stage, apart from to be aware of this, and to think about how their actions will impact on this

d) Start the measure

e) Start feeding back the results of the measure at meetings you already have

f) Over time: gain buy in and support from your people (you do this by using the information to catch your people doing something well, and by providing them with helpful information to improve sales that you glean from the customer feedback)

g) Make a large and prominent scoreboard (a good place to put this would be in your reception area and in your staff recreation area): be sure to change the score frequently (at the very least monthly). You can put other scores on this board (for example turnover or response times ... one or two key critical measures of your business), but don't make it busy – make it simple clear and empowering.

h) Start the go the extra inch meetings and start taking action from the results of those meetings.

i) Develop your communications so you have a process that drives greatness (as suggested in Chapter 7)

Then you'll have a SYSTEM to drive excellence and continuous improvement

For more advice and free information on this point, or to access paid help to make this work for you please go to *www.greatorpoorscore. com.*

11

ACTION

If you do anything from reading this book, consider doing the following:

- **Try clarifying your customer-focused mission:** start thinking about it, start discussing it in meetings and start making it work in your business.
- **Look at your systems and processes systematically.** Try and say to yourself: are these exceeding (or even meeting) my customers' REAL needs? Are these going to deliver great service? Are they going to build trust and make life easier for our customers? Do they make the customer feel valued? Will they make us systemically go the extra inch? Because if the answer to any of those is no, then 'great' customer experiences will not happen consistently and excellently.
- **Put an effective and empowering communications process in place** that will help you build 'greatness'. And stick to it like glue. (And stop having some of those boring and pointless meetings that you're 'always had'!)
- **Try to lead by example.** Whatever your role in the organisation, whether you're the chief executive or the newest employee, lead this stuff by example. Good examples are catching. You could have a huge effect. Just do it!
- **Empower people by teaching this material.** The best way to learn something is to teach it. You have everything here you need to enable you to do this. If you want extra information it's available at *www.greatorpoor.com* – register for our free newsletter and top tips or even send us an email, we'll help you. But, whatever your situation, start to teach this material to your people.*

- **Start scoring and having regular 'Go the Extra Inch' meetings!**
I think we've covered this enough already ...

Whatever you do, going forward from here, in the same way that you employ an Accountant to ensure you get your books right, *you need someone to make you stay on track with this*, you need a 'customer experience champion', and perhaps even a 'customer experience director'.

Whilst this is everyone's responsibility, it will help to have someone responsible for promulgating it and encouraging consistent actions and improvement. It will help even more to appoint an external coach (and, of course, we can help you with this) – you have to have someone to support you to make this work.

This is far too important to leave to chance.

And if you do leave it to chance I can guarantee you that 'normal life' will take over and most of this material will go out of the window.

This is a holistic approach:

- The customer experience comes from the actions that you take.
- Your actions derive from the processes and systems that you have in your head and in your organisation.
- Those processes and systems derive from the strategy in your head or your business.
- The strategy derives from beliefs: your personal beliefs, and the beliefs of the people who control your organisation.

If you believe this is 'too hard' or 'you haven't got time', you'll be right.

If you believe this is common sense and 'worth a try', you'll be right.

Let's hope you have the 2nd belief: *the essential thing is to make a start ... no matter how small.* Then keep reviewing and evolving.

It's ideal to work it the whole way through and take a completely holistic approach, but this may be too much to chew to start with.

Remember the following proverbs:

- No farmer ever ploughed his field by turning it over in his mind
- A journey of a thousand miles starts with the first step

Use the Japanese manufacturing technique of 'Kaizen': small steps, involving all people, resulting in continuous ongoing improvement, produces huge progress over time ... in fact, if you do it any other way, you'll just lurch about and have inconsistent progress (at best). Look at the diagram below – start at the top and then just keep going, using your regular 'Go the Extra Inch sessions' as your key driver (it's like riding a bike – you have to keep pedalling!)

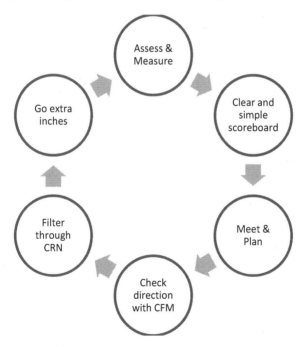

Don't worry, wherever you start, do it obsessively and with integrity because at least if you start something it will have an effect. If you don't start it and you give up it is only you that will suffer, it's your integrity that will take a bash.

There is further help available, go to *www.greatorpoor.com* you'll find free articles and an ongoing blog. Sign up and we'll send you free helpful tips on a weekly basis. We won't send you spam and rubbish, we'll just send you helpful stuff.

Contact us to see what other information we can send you for free or if we can help you on a paid basis. But please don't do nothing, because remember:

You are not in control of your business,
your customers are.

Whether you like it or not, your customers are already talking about you, either directly to their friends or, and of course now much more common and infinitely more powerful, on the internet and through social media.

The internet is empowering your customer unlike anything before or anything imaginable and it happens at the speed of light. You can either use this fact to your advantage or let it happen without you. Your business is now completely transparent ... and your CFM, and the behaviours it produces will ultimately determine what customers say about you to their friends.

Your challenge is to make sure that whatever is being said about you is 'great' on an ongoing basis. If you can achieve excellence in this area, word of mouth will market your business in a phenomenal way and deliver a stream of pre-sold leads and success to you.

If you don't, then you're skating on thin ice at best ... and, at worst, your customers can ruin your reputation overnight.

So please, don't do nothing. Look at your **customer-focused mission**, start using it as a compass for your activities, look at your **customer's real needs**, start using them as a filter for all systems, processes and actions, look at going the extra inch, start having the regular sessions – use these phrases in your organisation and please start measuring. Then and only then will you be able to become 'great' not 'poor'.

Very good luck to you.

APPENDIX 1

THE CUSTOMER SERVICE SWOT

<u>I am the greatest strength in your organisation</u>

... but I am often overlooked & ignored

I think you're 'OK' and I want to be your trusted friend, and a source of strength & growth

I can ensure your business thrives for years and years

Or I can drain you of energy and resources

All you need to do is to listen to me and change with my needs

... but you won't

... so I can't help you as I want to

I am your customer

If you don't pay attention to me, someone else will

I am the greatest weakness in your organisation

I am usually only 'satisfied' by you, and I am looking for something better

So when someone a little bit better comes along, I'll leave you

I don't want to do this

But you aren't truly focused on my needs and desires ... and your systems reflect this

... and you won't listen to me

So, as soon as I get a chance ... I'll go

And I'll weaken you until you perish

I am your customer

If you don't pay attention to me, someone else will

I am the greatest opportunity in your organisation

I want to help you build a truly great organisation ... for nothing!

And I cost very little to keep

In order to allow me to do this, you need to really value me and listen to me

But you don't seem to want to

So I can't help you nearly as much as I want to, and eventually I'll get fed up and stop trying

And you'll suffer from lack of ideas, and eventually you'll be unable to meet my needs for the future

So I'll go

I am your customer

If you don't pay attention to me, someone else will

I am the greatest threat to your organisation

If I think you're 'great', I'll tell a couple of my closest friends,

If you make a mistake, I won't tell you ... but I will tell everyone else

If I'm 'satisfied' , I'll stay with you only until someone else grabs my attention (which is not very long)

My deepest desire is to be your friend and partner

I want to trust you and make both our lives easier

... but you won't listen to me

I can ruin your business overnight: history shows countless times when I've done this

I am your customer

If you don't pay attention to me, someone else will

APPENDIX 2

HOW TO LOSE CUSTOMERS AND ALIENATE PEOPLE

Top Tips to annoy your customers and fail

1. Believe that good products and services will sell themselves: you don't want to get tied up in all that messy selling business
2. Believe that you are in business to make money: any other belief is foolish
3. Think that the best way to make money out of people is to give the minimum service at the maximum margin you can get away with
4. Develop products and services that are unique, and then sit on your laurels and charge through your nose for them: by the time people catch up with you, you'll have made enough money
5. Think that your life will be much easier and less stressful without clients or customers: they are just a pain in the neck
6. Believe that the only way to win is to be the cheapest
7. Whatever you do, don't plan: never make any to do list, never follow up enquiries routinely, and just hope that people will pester you if they need it badly enough
8. Never respond to business enquiries quickly: you have many more important tasks
9. Always avoid complaints: complainers are just a pain in the neck and will waste your time: they never have anything useful to tell you
10. Always be too busy to return phone calls: if it's important they'll phone you back
11. If you're a qualified professional, remember you don't need to worry about this customer services nonsense: you've spent years

qualifying and they should pay you because of your expertise

12. Remember that the secret of selling is not to listen to the customer and find out what they really want, but to hoodwink them with your expertise and sell them something that sounds good and makes you a lot of money

13. Promote your goods and services first around what makes you the most money: forget what's most valuable to the customer ... if they really are that interested they'll find out

14. In order to get better at selling you need to go on a sales course that will teach you how to close sales and pressurise people into making decisions before they're ready

15. Always try and hide your prices: never publish them transparently ... customers might find out!

16. Be sure to be embarrassed about your prices or fees: always offer hefty discounts before anyone questions you on your prices

17. Never look for ways to deliver the same or better results for less money: this is commercial suicide

18. Always look for ways to add on hidden extras and fees that your customer is not expecting, so you can make more money out of each person

19. Under no circumstances give a money back guarantee: all customers are crooks and will take you for a ride

20. Always think your service is the best and ridicule your competition: never look for ways to improve it

21. Never do customer surveys or listen to your customers ... they'll tell you things that are awkward to hear

22. What do the customers know anyway? You're the expert, they should listen to you more.

23. Always give a quote by letter: making long winded and confusing so you sound impressive. Under no circumstances make it short and easy to deal with or your customers might be able to compare your services to your competition's

24. Always leave the next move to the customer: use phrases like 'if I can be of any further service please don't hesitate to contact me'

25. Never follow leads up actively, this is pushy and beneath you

26. When you're selling to someone, make sure you tell them how fantastic your company is and make sure that you don't forget to

tell them about all the features and benefits of your product or service ... don't waste time listening to them!

27. Never listen to find out what customers real needs are: you're the expert, you need to tell them what they should want even if they don't

28. When you're talking with customers or potential customers, make sure to tell them all about yourself and to regale them with stories that you want to tell ... whatever you do, however, be sure to avoid listening to their problems and issues

29. Spend loads of money on marketing and advertising ... and then sit and wait for the customers to find you

30. Never ask customers for feedback: potential customers aren't interested in what people really think of you, just blind them with your brilliance in marketing and sales come

31. With your marketing, focus on your brand and your products and services: definitely do not include anything that shows the results that people might like all want

32. Develop a reputation for being unreliable: you're very busy, so customers shouldn't expect you to return calls when you say you will or turn up at the time you promised

33. Make wild promises with your marketing: customers won't remember, so you won't have to honour them, you just need to sound impressive so customers ring you

34. Never ever meet with your people to discuss what you could do better to deliver better customer experiences, it's a waste of time, they'll just try and screw you for more pay

35. Treat your people as idiots: they are not nearly as brilliant as you, so they're going to be rubbish at looking after customers unless you on their backs all the time

36. Don't empower people: they'll throw it back in your face

37. Make sure all your systems and processes are designed to stop your people and your customers stealing from you: the best way to make money is not to lose money

38. Remember to be a strong leader: this means telling people what to do in a blunt fashion, and then shouting at them if they get any tiny bit wrong

39. If you can't do this, be nice to people, and don't tell them when

they get things wrong as you might hurt their feelings: just hope that they'll get better over time if you don't say anything

40. Make sure your systems and processes focus on saving your company money and time: under no circumstances have systems and processes that are designed to make it easy for the customer because they might well make it harder for you

41. Never thank people for doing good things catch them doing something well: they should be doing this anyway and don't need you to thank them

42. Remember that money is more important than anything all the time: change processes and principles to make money at the drop of a hat ... that's what you're in business for!

43. Have lots of signs saying that you value the customer: but don't bother to put a system in place to listen to them, because they only whinge and cause you problems

APPENDIX 3

HOW TO HANDLE COMPLAINTS

I recently had 2 complaints with 2 different companies that have been handled in 2 different ways with 2 different outcomes.

First complaint was with a phone supplier. The complaint was handled in an OK way by the operative on the phone, but I was unhappy about a number of aspects and their system as a whole, and so I asked for a Manager to give me a ring. This was promised to me, but, despite 2 more reminders from me, has never happened.

I will now stop trading with this Company as soon as I can.

The second complaint was with a power Company over a gas bill wrongly charged. Again the complaint was handled in an OK way by the operative on the phone, but I was once more unhappy about the process and asked for a Manager to call me.

Two days later I had a call from a Manager in the complaints department who couldn't get through to me but left me their name and direct phone number. I was able to call them back 2 days later and the phone went straight through to this person. They listened to my complaint, agreed that the process was flawed, assured me that they would get the process changed and offered me on the spot a compensatory figure (not very much ... it doesn't have to be ... it's the caring that counts, not the money). And I was left feeling cared for, appreciated, and listened to.

The result is, I will stay loyal to this company whenever I can, and they have learnt ways that their process can be improved.

WIN WIN!

How you handle complaints is critically important.

Handle them well, and you will find ways to improve your process again and again and again, and, at the same time, create loyal customers who promote your business with their friends and colleagues.

Handle them badly and you not only lose customers, but you also lose vital steps in your continued evolution and improvement.

Over time, if this process is repeated, you will go out of business. Here's a really simple Guide:

a) **Customer-Focused Mission:** your purpose is to do something so well that people want to pay you – complaints are an essential source of helpful information to help you do this. A complaint badly handled can seriously harm your organization … on the other hand, handled well can be a source of true and loyal customers.

   – Deal with complaints as if they were 'compliments': indeed why not get your whole organization to adopt this change of wording!

   – Empower all your people to be able to deal with any complaints directly without recourse to someone else: empowered people generally feel compelled to act responsibly … and unempowered people generally don't!

   – Look for 'hidden complaints': through body language, tone of voice, returned goods, changes of customer behavior, and be very proactive to address them.

   – Train and empower everyone to spot and deal with these confidently.

   – Offer guarantees and service charters, and publicise them as widely as possible.

b) **Customer's REAL needs:** the customer has 3 REAL needs

   – Attention: start off with an apology that they have had to bring this to your attention – whether you think this complaint is genuine or not! Then give them time and listen to them with integrity – ask them clarifying questions to find out the REAL issue, and why they feel upset enough to complain to you (remember, most people won't complain, they'll just tell their friends instead).

   – Easier or better life: communicate and listen empathically until you can find out what they REALLY require as a resolution and what actions they REALLY want from you.

Never guess or leap to conclusion; always communicate excellently until you understand their REAL needs and expectations (which may well be very different from what you think). Then ensure that a problem is fixed QUICKLY. This will make the customer's life easier.
- Trust: Tell them what you're going to do by when and how they'll know. Reiterate your service charters and Guarantees. Give out direct line telephone numbers. Make it easy for them to come back to you. And then contact them again, as appropriate, when you've done what you said you would.

c) Go the Extra Inch:
- Do the above to meet the customers' needs,
- Then perhaps add a little extra on the end to thank the customer for bringing this to your attention.
- Then go a further inch to address the issue that caused the complaint in the first place
- Then ensure everyone knows all about it

d) Measure:
- Number of complaints
- Subject of complaints: (person / department / process)
- Time of complaints
- Time to resolution
- Etc etc
- Then meet regularly, probably in your 'Go the Extra Inch' meetings, to review complaints and ensure you've taken the appropriate actions to make sure both the individual complaint and the issue that caused it have been rectified properly.